Building
Team
Resilience

 **WWR**

Kathryn McEwen

First published 2016
Second published 2017 by
Mindset Publications

ISBN 978-0-646-96118-7

Designed by Aled McEwen.
Layout and printing by Openbook Howden Print & Design
St Marys, South Australia 5042

This book is dedicated to members of my family, who at the time of writing, were on major journeys of resilience. To my sister Jane who has taken advanced cancer head-on and fought through it; to my father Bill who is also battling cancer without fuss; and to my mother Jean who has worked through the health and grief issues of ageing with the 'you have to just get on with it' attitude she and dad have gifted to us, their children.

And finally to my husband Allan who has faced his own resilience challenges, including marriage!

About the Author

Kathryn McEwen is an organisational psychologist, company director and executive coach who specialises in optimising leader, team and organisational performance. It is her passion to help create workplaces that simultaneously create high performance, personal enjoyment and well-being.

Kathryn has a particular interest in workplace resilience and leads *Working With Resilience*, an international consortium of professionals interested in assessing and building resilience at work.

Ensuring a strong evidence-base to her work, Kathryn collaborates with the University of South Australia through lecturing, student placements and membership of advisory committees. She is sought after as a speaker at industry conferences and has been recognised for her contribution to the psychology profession by being awarded the status of Fellow by the Australian Psychological Society.

In this book she draws on her wealth of experience in coaching leaders and groups. At one end of the spectrum this has involved working to create high performance, and at the other assisting to restore performance. Her extensive hands-on knowledge of behaviour and organisational change, team dynamics, leadership, psychological well-being, work performance and mediation is integrated into the book.

Kathryn and her team consult widely to corporate, government and not-for-profit organisations to assist leaders and teams build employee and team resilience.

This book was inspired by the many conversations with clients about their need to build the capacity of their leaders and teams to perform, adapt and thrive in the uncertainty and pressures inherent in work today.

Reach Kathryn and her colleagues at www.workingwithresilience.com.au.

Table of Contents

Acknowledgements

Many people have helped develop this book and the model that underlies it, however some deserve special thanks:

- Dr. Carolyn Boyd for providing statistical and methodological expertise in developing the Resilience at Work (R@W) Team
- Rochelle Colon for her conscientiousness and attention to detail in the research assistance roles she has played
- Emily Lawrie for assistance in proof reading and statistical analysis
- Aled McEwen for the book's layout and design
- Allan McEwen Junior for his support in IT and promotion
- Antionette Rodighiero for her advice and assistance in shaping the first drafts of what became two books
- Carol Duncan for insights from a coach and manager perspective
- Steve Kilcoyne for his design skills in developing graphics for the models
- Allan McEwen, my husband, who always stands beside me in my work and supported me in writing yet another book.

And of course to the many leaders and teams I have learned from who took the risk to employ me to 'experiment' on them.

About this book

Building Team Resilience is of value if your team is looking for sustainable ways to manage a challenging working environment. You and your colleagues may be:

- Re-building after a major restructure or changes in staffing or organisational direction
- Regularly dealing with difficult tasks or demanding customers
- Working in constant change and uncertainty
- Experiencing difficult group dynamics

2

- Time pressured or having to do more with less
- Trying to meet unrealistic or competing demands from your Board or Executive Team
- On track but looking for an extra boost to your team effectiveness.

This book will help you develop a team resilience plan for your particular circumstances. It is designed for team members looking to implement ideas with colleagues, as well as for leaders seeking ideas for their staff.

Within it, the author draws on her research into workplace resilience, direct experience in resilience-building interventions and established theoretical models. Concepts within the positive psychology, occupational stress, change and organisational behaviour fields of research are integrated into practical advice that can be implemented by any team.

The combination of good theory and expert practice provides a workable blueprint for any type of team. The framework can be applied to most occupations and industry sectors, and for groups at all levels.

The ideas will assist you if you want your team to perform optimally at work while keeping personal well-being intact over the longer-term. Your work may be inherently physically or emotionally challenging - such as emergency and community services. Or, on the other hand, you may have everyday types of jobs but the workload pressure and expectations on your team are high. Regardless of your challenges, building resilience can assist you to collectively adapt to changing circumstances, optimise your performance and then sustain it.

How to use this book

Building Team Resilience focuses on developing a customised plan for building resilience within your team.

It is best used in conjunction with the author's book *Building Your Resilience: How to Thrive in a Challenging Job* (Appendix B) that focuses on techniques to develop personal resilience.

Throughout the book, you and your colleagues are encouraged to complete a number of reflective exercises and combine these to form a team resilience plan. To create ownership, it is best for you to work together and identify shared actions.

As you work through the text, you will find that the introduction and Chapter 1 provide the context for why we need resilience in our working life, while Chapters 2 and 3 introduce the R@W Team model used throughout. On completing an initial assessment of your current team's resilience in Chapter 4, you can explore each of the seven components in detail in Chapters 5 to 11, identifying strategies that may work for you. In Chapter 12 you then have the opportunity to pull together the ideas that resonate for you into a team plan.

If you hold a leadership position, Chapter 13 provides a number of reflective questions to assess the extent to which you are leading in a way that supports resilience within your group.

While it is best to work through the book systematically, Chapters 5 to 11 each focus on a specific component of team resilience and so allow you to dip in quickly and explore aspects that are of more interest to you.

In order to illustrate and bring the ideas to life there are case studies throughout the book. Quick Quips within the text are also provided that give humorous or insightful commentary on topics. These are comments heard by the author and her colleagues in their work.

The approach advocated in the book can be used multiple times as your plan may need to be reviewed and updated as work circumstances change.

| Introduction

Why resilience at work?

Resilience has become a buzzword in all aspects of our lives. We talk about it in communities, in parenting children, in creating sustainable environments, in recovering from traumatic or difficult events – and more recently in managing challenging jobs and volatile working conditions.

Within workplaces resilience has also become an imperative as the landscape of our work has and will continue to shift dramatically, with constant change, higher workloads and expectations together with increasing complexity. These changes demand different ways of working that allow us to perform optimally while staying well, both physically and emotionally. They require actions that allow us to be both agile and able to sustain our performance and well-being over the longer-term.

The difficult working conditions we experience affect us personally but also impact on the groups in which we operate. This means that our attention to team dynamics and effectiveness needs to intensify in order to collaboratively manage challenges, rather than take them on individually. While we need to continue to pay attention to well-established elements of teamwork such as clear goals and responsibilities there are areas emerging that need additional attention in order to ensure sustainable performance. How we work collectively to build and retain the resilience of our team is the focus of this book.

The main drivers for resilience

Teams are facing the challenges of frequent change, increased workload and more demanding customers. They are often required to work in environments that are uncertain and ambiguous, and on tasks that are becoming more complex.

An acronym related to these shifts that is creeping into the vocabulary in leadership circles is VUCA. It stands for:

- Volatile
- Uncertain
- Complex
- Ambiguous.

Borrowed from the military, VUCA describes what is now being considered as the new normal operating environment for many organisations.

Before exploring how resilience can assist it is important, however, to outline in more detail the challenges that resilience is being asked to address.

The rise of change and uncertainty

Few teams can now escape regular changes in the environment in which they operate – whether it's technological advances, transformed organisational structures and business markets or simply regular changes in staffing, leadership or work processes. Often the change produces periods of uncertainty where we may worry about employment contracts being renewed, how our job might change, or even if the organisation itself will survive. Such change also involves planning and implementation time that detracts from the time spent performing the activities inherent in our positions. This turbulence can impact on the performance and even the viability of our team.

Quick Quip

"Management keep saying it's business as usual but how can it be when we are in the middle of a restructure and still don't know who is staying and who is losing their jobs."

Quick Quip

"We have had a revolving door of executives and each implements a new structure while we continue to provide the same service we always have. It creates a lot of turmoil and uncertainty for little gain."

Quick Quip

"The reception role has been automated and we are now obsolete."

Managing workload and customer expectations

As well as needing to adapt to change there may be increasing expectations on our performance. Customers, managers and stakeholders demand we deliver more in shorter time timeframes, with fewer resources. People commonly complain that they have declining budgets and fewer resources but the same, and often much more, to do. The hackneyed phrase 'work smarter not harder' that was used so often a decade ago now creates anger as employees see it as a reflection on their lack of effort or skills rather than recognition of the unrelenting demands on them.

The public, through courtesy of the internet, are more educated and likely to have firm opinions on what they want. Customer expectations that haven't been met can add to pressure. Anger and abuse directed towards front-line staff is on the increase as members of the public are now more likely to assert their rights, voice their dissatisfaction and sometimes personalise discontent. This is often in jobs where emotional labour is already high such as call centres, service counters, schools and hospital emergency departments.

The overall result can be team conflict and disharmony, as well as increasing absenteeism or turnover.

Quick Quip

"People used to be thankful for a free mammogram, now they complain we're running late, they can't get a car park outside of the door or it hurts too much." (Radiographer).

Quick Quip

"Some of my patients are coming in having self-diagnosed through research on the internet. Sometimes they tell me what medication to prescribe." (General practitioner).

Increasing complexity and ambiguity

While change and workloads are obvious key drivers in requests for resilience, complexity is also an emerging influence with more and more factors to consider when making decisions. Risk management, business continuity, protecting the corporate image on social media and legal and human resource compliance are just a small sample of the requirements team members can have responsibility for. All this adds to an already busy day and long working hours. In this environment teams can feel they no longer add real value and can get caught up in processes rather than outcomes.

Quick Quip

"If we spent as much time with our clients as we do proving we are compliant with our funding requirements we'd be a lot more effective."

Quick Quip

"Almost everything I do impacts on other teams so I spend a lot of my time influencing and consulting rather than designing."

Now that we have outlined the problems we want resilience to solve, we can explore what resilience is.

| Notes

Chapter 1

Exploring team resilience

What is this concept called resilience?

Resilience is complex and multi-faceted. It is similar to a lot of other constructs we talk about creating in organisations such as good leadership and teamwork. We know what it looks like, and what it doesn't look like, but when we attempt to unpack how to create it we find it isn't easy.

Adding to the confusion are the numerous definitions of resilience. Central to most of these though is the notion that resilience involves being able to withstand and overcome adversity and unpleasant or difficult events successfully and to be able to adapt to change and uncertainty.

Can we become more resilient?

While it is acknowledged that there are aspects of our personality that lead to resilience, there is now consensus that it is a dynamic process that can be developed in most of us and is subject to change. This means that while some people may have more resilient personal characteristics, such as optimism and flexibility, we can all learn and develop the thoughts and behaviours that underpin resilience. It also means that our levels of resilience may shift in accordance with the particular challenges we are facing and how we are thinking about and responding to these. If resilience is a state rather than a fixed personality trait it means two things:

- We can develop our resilience, and
- We need to regularly review and maintain the actions and thoughts that support our resilience as our circumstances change.

We can apply these principles to ourselves and also to the teams in which we operate.

"Why do we need resilience training? We are still here despite the market conditions so we must be resilient." (Comment by a senior executive).

How do we define work resilience?

Defining what we mean by resilience in the work context is important given the variability in descriptors. We define it as:

The capacity to manage the everyday stress of work and remain healthy, rebound and learn from unexpected setbacks and prepare for future challenges proactively.

Our definition builds on the traditional elements of overcoming adversity and being adaptable to change to also include a proactive element of preparing for future challenges through anticipation and innovation.

As a team is made up of a group of individuals then each person within it needs to display the capabilities implicit in this definition.

If we translate the definition of personal resilience to one that applies at a team-level, we can describe it as:

The capacity of a group of employees to collectively manage the everyday pressure of work and remain healthy, to adapt to change and to be proactive in positioning for future challenges.

The three interrelated elements inherent in our definition of team resilience - mastering stress, adapting to change and being proactive are shown graphically in Figure 1.

Figure 1: Elements of Work Resilience

Dispelling the myths around resilience

Within workplaces building resilience is sometimes perceived as a covert strategy to get people to take on more load and pressure. However, as the definition above implies, resilience is also about agility and best positioning yourself and your team for the next inevitable challenge or setback. In essence it is being the best you can be, both individually and collectively, in the environment in which you work. It is not just about managing stress but also about remaining relevant.

Quick Quip

"This resilience thing is just a con to get our members to work harder." (Union official).

Another common misunderstanding is that resilience is an attribute needed only by teams who are under-performing. The reality is, however, that attention to resilience is important for us all. As outlined, our resilience levels are dynamic and change according to how we respond to what we are experiencing in our environment. This means we need to regularly review and track how we are travelling. If we are managing relatively well, we still need to attend to how we maintain what we are doing.

Finally, resilience should not be confused with stoicism or heroism. While persistence is important, continuing to push ahead despite the impact on your team's relationships, health or reputation is highly detrimental.

In the next chapter we will discuss how each member of our group needs to invest in their personal resilience but that this alone does not create resilience within a team. The latter involves collective effort and alignment. The actions involved are explored within the framework of the Resilience at Work (R@W) Team model.

⚙ Top Tips

Be clear in your definition of work resilience

Resilience is complex and means different things to different people. In the workplace we are using it as the answer to problems we face when working in VUCA environments. The definition and approach we use needs to reflect this need rather than duplicate other areas where resilience is important such as community disasters, mental health and general well-being and happiness.

Resilience is a work in progress

Our resilience is a dynamic state so we can develop it but it also needs regular review and maintenance as our circumstances change. We cannot claim it as a permanent trait of our team.

Resilience is about sustaining optimal performance not coping better

A common mistake at work is seeing resilience as an attribute needed by teams who are under-performing, change resistant or simply 'not up to the job.' While we need to ensure we have strategies to manage everyday pressures and adapt to change, resilience also includes awareness of strengths and positioning to be the best we can be. At the other end of the spectrum resilience is not about persisting despite the negative impact on health and relationships. Stoicism is not resilience.

Chapter 2

Introducing the R@W® Team model

What is team resilience?

Being resilient at work is about creating sustainable success rather than coping over the short-term. Within a team it is multi-faceted and involves the capacity to:

- Create a climate that promotes cohesion and also allows members to manage the pressures of work while staying physically and mentally healthy
- Adapt to change and collectively respond and learn from unexpected setbacks such as changes in job role, workload or working arrangements
- Be proactive and anticipate and position for future challenges together.

To achieve these capabilities as a team we all need to take responsibility for our personal resilience as each of us has an impact on the team's overall dynamic and performance. However, investing in the resilience of individual members alone will not guarantee a resilient team. We also need alignment with those we work with.

As an example, a sense of purpose, having support and being able to engage in self-care activities are all part of what we need to invest in personally to be resilient. However, if the team differs on purpose, is non-supportive with each other and does not promote well-being, our resilience can be shaken, or even decimated.

In this section we use the R@W Team model as a framework for understanding the actions needed at a team level.

Origins of the R@W® Team model

The R@W Team model has been designed specifically for groups who work in challenging jobs. It explores the everyday actions that teams can take to build optimal performance at work while maintaining well-being.

The model is based on the R@W Team Scale, a measure of team resilience researched and developed in 2015 by the book's author and research psychologist, Dr. Carolyn Boyd (Appendix A).

Research for the Scale was developed out of substantial experience in working with leaders and teams who operate in challenging environments, as well as research on work resilience.

Uses of the R@W® Team model

You can use the model to restore, build or maintain the resilience of your team through investing in its seven components as shown in Figure 2. How you do this is described in detail in Chapter 3.

Figure 2: R@W® Team Model

The value of a model

Having a visual model such as this provides an easy to understand overview of the factors needed to build a complex concept like team resilience. It also creates a common language for workplace conversations and interventions. While the components appear simple, each can open up a rich conversation around approaches and activities.

The R@W® Toolkit

The R@W Team is part of a broader toolkit of three resilience measures as shown in Figure 3 and outlined in Appendix A.

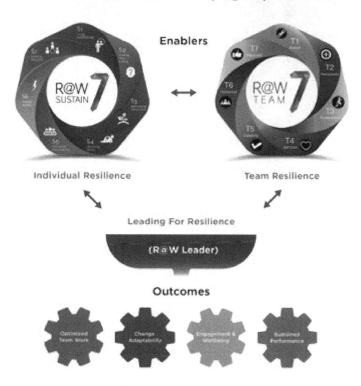

Figure 3: The R@W® Toolkit

The importance of a systemic approach

Building our team resilience requires changing our thoughts and actions. Within a workplace, as in communities, sustainable change requires a systemic approach that considers the interrelationship of the elements that influence our thoughts and actions. As shown in Figure 4 this means considering how individual, team and organisational factors, as well as external influences such as the economy, market conditions and customer expectations, impact on one another.

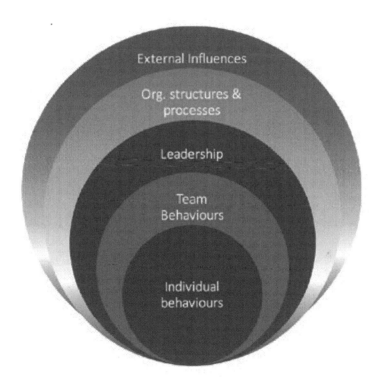

Figure 4: The Organisation as a System

Individual level factors

Most approaches to resilience building at work seem to focus on the employee. This is perhaps because much of the research in this area derives from clinical and positive psychology, which tends to focus more on individuals.

There is no doubt that we are all accountable for our performance and contribution to the team, and if all of us work on our levels of resilience it will make a considerable difference. The team we work with and the leader we report to can, however, promote or detract from our resilience. As a result, a focus on individuals alone can limit the sustainability of any changes we attempt to make.

The R@W Scale (Individual) in Appendix A outlines the components required at a personal level.

Team level factors

Resilience at a team level is not simply the sum of the resilience of each member. In the same way that a group of champions does not necessarily produce a champion team, a resilient group of people does not guarantee a resilient team.

Collectively we need to develop an environment that fosters resilience. This includes aspects such as creating shared purpose, mutual support and accountability. Without this alignment and cooperation, we can work against, rather than for, the resilience of those we work with.

We also need to promptly attend to counter-productive behaviours as these can quickly impact on resilience. Adding a new employee to the team who has a different value set or agenda from everyone else is an all too common example of this.

Leader level factors

If you are employed as a manager, you have a substantial impact on your team given the additional influence and authority assigned to your role. This means you can promote, or detract from, resilience through both your personal role modelling and your support for actions that foster team resilience. Whether you want to, or not, you directly influence the workplace climate and the unwritten rules of how things operate within your team.

An example would be where flexible work practices are available but are not supported by the leader due to a lack of trust that people can self-manage their workload. This in turn can impact on a team's capacity to manage stress.

Quick Quip

"Whether or not you get to use the company's flexible working arrangements depends on the manager you work for."

Actively promoted here is the belief that leaders should combine personal resilience with humanity. Unfortunately, there are too many leaders who are resilient in spite of others. You may know of someone who seems to have climbed the organisational ladder despite the negative impact they have on those around them. Their self-interest, rather than the common good, drives their resilience and their style can be destructive for the teams they lead.

The R@W Leader (Appendix A), outlines desired leader actions for building team resilience and is explored later in Chapter 13.

Organisation level factors

At an organisational level we need to establish systems, processes and structures that support employee, team and leadership actions. When protocols work against the team behaviours required they can prevent change occurring. A common example would be attempting to develop shared team goals when individual key performance indicators or employment contracts are in competition with these.

Teams often feel powerless in influencing organisational practices, yet part of creating workplace resilience is educating leaders and teams on the prerequisites for resilience so that they can 'manage up' and positively advocate for change. People sometimes underestimate the capacity to influence upwards.

A large number of incremental changes can make a big difference to your team. These can also be more sustainable as members have a sound understanding of the operational requirements that make them viable and develop a sense of ownership around implementation.

The concept of organisational resilience

This book focuses on the resilience of people in the workplace. This is quite different from the resilience of the organisation itself.

There is sometimes a tendency to refer to organisational resilience as though it is the same construct as personal resilience. Organisational resilience however depends on the extent to which an organisation can survive and prosper by anticipating and responding to unexpected events and change. Market restructuring, cyber safety, technology innovations and climate change are just some of the aspects that can have a major impact on operational viability. Consideration around these aspects often forms part of an organisation's business continuity, security and risk management plans.

The term organisational resilience is also used in crisis and emergency management, and in disaster recovery, to describe the capacity to respond to sudden and major disruption.

Other important areas to consider are organisational structures and processes and the capacity to be nimble and quickly realign or respond to changing circumstances.

To summarise, if we want to create resilience at a group level we need to build the personal resilience of members but also consider what the team and leader can do to support these efforts. We also need to consider how teams can influence the organisational structures and processes required to support their efforts.

⚙ Top Tips

Differentiate between team and individual resilience

The resilience of a team is not the collective sum of the resilience of its members. It is built through group activities that both foster and align the actions of people. We need to invest in building the resilience of both the individual and the team.

Take a systems approach

Sustainable behaviour change at work is created through understanding the interrelationship between employees, teams, leaders and organisational structures and processes. Investing in each of these areas is important when building resilience.

Use a visual model

Having a visual framework or model to illustrate a complex construct like resilience is helpful as it provides a workplace communication tool as well as a mechanism to make sense of the complexity of variables underpinning resilience.

Recognise that resilient employees do not necessarily create a resilient organisation

An organisation cannot rely solely on the resilience of its people to be nimble and survive in a turbulent operating environment. While leaders and staff can influence decisions that impact on this, there are a multitude of other factors that need to be considered when considering business survival.

| Notes

Chapter 3

The 7 components of the R@W® Team

The R@W® Team model

In this chapter we introduce the R@W Team. The seven components of the model, as shown in Figure 5, interrelate and contribute to our overall team resilience.

Figure 5: R@W® Team Model

Exploring the 7 R@W® Team components

To be resilient a team needs to be competent. It still needs to perform well in all of the elements that we know contribute to effectiveness.

Aspects such as having a shared direction, clear roles and responsibilities, talent, open communication and good leadership are all examples of elements long established as necessary for teamwork. These elements remain important and are incorporated into the R@W Team model. Also included in the model however are activities that are now emerging as *additional* qualities that are needed when employed in challenging jobs.

For example, as workloads increase, the capacity to look after the health of employees requires more focus. As budgets remain the same or are cut, with no corresponding reduction in services, we need to better optimise the resources we have and build our capacity through linking into external advice and supports. When morale is at risk through uncertainty and unexpected setbacks we need to persist and remain positive. All these are examples of some of the attributes that have become more prominent as work becomes more difficult. To build resilience, teams need to attend to these emerging factors as well as those well established as contributing to teamwork.

A brief overview of the seven R@W components is summarised as follows.

T1 Robust
Having shared purpose, goals and values and the skills needed to do the job. Being proactive when issues arise for the team.

T2 Resourceful

Harnessing team member strengths
and resources and building a culture of
continuous improvement. Developing effective
team processes that enable a clear focus on priorities.

T3 Perseverance

Staying optimistic and having a solution, rather than
a problem, focus. Persisting in the face of obstacles.

T4 Self-care

Promoting and deploying good stress management
routines and being alert to overload in members.
Supporting life-work balance.

T5 Capability

Continually building capacity
through accessing networks and supports.
Seeking feedback and building on what works well.

T6 Connected	
	Caring for colleagues as people and being co-operative and supportive with each other.

T7 Alignment	
	Aligning and developing the talents of team members to create the desired outcomes. Sharing and celebrating success with each other.

The Impact of factors outside of the team

As advocated in Chapter 2, a systemic approach to creating behaviour change advocates that actions at the team level need to be supported by organisational policy and processes. Recognition of team effort and success, for example, can be reinforced through a formal reward and recognition program, while shared team values should align with corporate values.

While ensuring organisation-wide policies to support team actions is strongly promoted here, this book focuses on activities and approaches that are generally within the scope of the team itself to implement or influence.

In the next chapter you can start to explore the current state of resilience within your team and what you may need to do to maintain or enhance it.

⚙ Top Tips

Understand how team resilience builds on teamwork

Teams still need to engage in the activities known to create effective teamwork. However, the advent of VUCA working environments has created additional factors that need attention to ensure resilience.

Chapter 4

Assessing your current team resilience

Developing a team plan

In this chapter you can start to formulate a plan to build your team resilience through a number of steps:

Step 1: Noting what you currently do that creates resilience and then mapping these identified actions against the R@W Team model components.

Step 2: Rating the team's overall performance in each of the seven components.

Step 3: Starting to formulate a plan by determining both team strengths and areas worth further exploration.

How to get started

Step 1: Identify what the team already does well

If your team's role is challenging, then it is likely that you already have a number of ways to manage pressure and unexpected challenges.

The first step in developing your plan is to identify what you do already that is working well.

These strengths may not be obvious, as sometimes the elements that create a resilient team are not recognised until they disappear. A good example of this is strong strategic external networks (capability) that can be lost, either suddenly through the turnover of key personnel, or over a longer period of time when not enough attention has been dedicated to relationship building. Until these networks are missing the team may not realise how important they are.

Recognising what you are already doing effectively is useful as it prompts more conscious attention to retaining these actions. In addition, it is always easier to build on strengths than do something quite different.

In the table below, list the actions your team takes, or the ways in which members respond, that help you all get through a difficult task, day or week at work. Examples could be encouraging time out after a difficult event, or actions that help the team gain perspective or link into external supports.

Once you have done this task identify the component of the R@W Team model that each activity seems to relate to. For example, de-briefing with each other relates to 'connected', while taking a lunch break and eating is 'self-care'. Indicate the related component within the table.

Exercise – Identifying our current actions

Activities	The R@W Team component this activity relates to

Activities	The R@W Team component this activity relates to

Step 2: Rate your team on the 7 components

For the second step rate your team from 0-6 on how well you think you invest in each of the seven components, with 0 being not at all and 6 being always. Do not reflect too long on this, as intuitive judgement works best.

If you have undertaken the R@W Team Scale (Appendix A), you can place your score in the rating column rather than make an estimate.

Once you have rated the components then explain your scores by stating what led you to rate the team in that way. The 'why' element is especially important as it prompts you to reflect on what is going well and what isn't. An example is provided in the table below.

You can do this activity individually and then discuss your thoughts, or work together as a team.

Example – team rating on components

R@W Team Component	Rating 0-6 or R@W Team Scale rating	What led me/us to rate the team in this way
Robust	3	We have a clear strategic direction and goals as well as great talent within the team but egos and personal agendas often get in the way.
Resourceful	6	We are very good at putting our energy into the things that matter and constantly look at improving how we operate.
Perseverance	4	Most members stay positive and keep persisting despite the major challenges we are facing. We have less energy at the moment due to meeting a major project deadline.
Self-care	3	We are all able to work well under pressure but the workload is high and life-work balance suffers. I think we are seeing the signs of people becoming unwell but no one is saying anything as they don't want to be seen as not coping.
Capability	6	We have great industry networks that we tap into and we spend a lot of energy on getting customer feedback on our performance. We each have a mentor or coach.
Connected	1	There is not a lot of co-operation or caring in the team. We do not spend much time socialising or taking an interest in each other as people. I don't feel any particular commitment to the team itself. It feels a little like 'dog eats dog'.
Alignment	2	There is a lot of competitiveness within the team that prevents knowledge sharing. People concentrate on their own targets and ambitions – sometimes at the cost of others.

Exercise – Rating your team on the R@W Team components

R@W Team Component	Rating 0-6 or R@W Team Scale rating	What led me/us to rate the team in this way
Robust		
Resourceful		

41

R@W Team Component	Rating 0-6 or R@W Team Scale rating	What led me/us to rate the team in this way
Perseverance		
Self-care		

R@W Team Component	Rating 0-6 or R@W Team Scale rating	What led me/us to rate the team in this way
Capability		
Connected		

R@W Team Component	Rating 0-6 or R@W Team Scale rating	What led me/us to rate the team in this way
Alignment		

Step 3: Start to formulate a resilience plan

After completing the above steps you should now have some sense of how well your team is tracking in regard to their investment in each of the seven components of the model.

In order to start developing your resilience plan you now need to:

- Build on, or at least maintain, the strengths that you have identified.
- Address areas that need more attention.

The remaining chapters of this book share ideas that will assist in this.

Making changes stick

Changing team behaviour is difficult. One person can rarely drive it. You need commitment and energy from enough members to build a degree of momentum, and in small teams just one or two people can be major blockers.

Also, while your goals may seem straightforward, achieving them is not necessarily easy. Some aspects to consider when initiating changes are outlined below.

Visualise what you would like the team to look like

Having a clear vision of what you want as a team can help guide your actions. What does it feel like when your team is at its most resilient? What is said? What is overcome? What do the relationships look like? How are changes initiated? How are people supported in who they are and what they are doing?

Try undertaking a group visualisation and sharing the images that people experience. Knowing where you want to be is the essential starting point for any change. Visualising what it looks and feels like can motivate you to achieve it.

Specific visualisations for each of the R@W Team components are provided in Chapter 13.

Build on what is working already

Building on existing successful strategies is always easier than developing new ones. Perhaps, for example, when things go wrong you take a two-minute break or de-brief with a colleague. It may be that when co-workers are ill there is an immediate regrouping to discuss priorities and share the additional workload. Part of your plan should be to identify how positive actions you currently take can be maintained during busy periods, or used more often.

Remember small shifts are more sustainable

If your team is already under pressure, then having the time and energy to make major changes is unrealistic. However, small shifts in a number of areas can make a significant difference. These are more manageable and often more sustainable longer term. If these are strategic, that is they address important gaps or maintain critical actions, then the small adjustments can have an even more significant impact.

As shifts become embedded as habits they become easier to maintain when the pressure is on. An obvious example is self-care strategies that are often the first to go when job demands increase. A pre-scheduled fortnightly shared lunch that ensures people eat something, as well as catch up on what is happening, is one example of an action that can become part of a team's routine. If it is planned and attendance is encouraged, it is less subject to disruption by other priorities.

Invest in multiple strategies

To build a good level of overall team resilience, it is best to invest in each of the seven R@W Team components, although not necessarily equally.

By developing capabilities, as much as you can, in each of the components, your team will increase its capacity to manage challenges, as well as adapt and prepare for uncertainty and change.

Recognise that a significant gap in one aspect of the R@W Team model can overshadow the team's strengths and even create disharmony and dysfunction. As an example, we know that pursuit of individual agendas by members, when there is fierce competition or a lack of shared values (robust), can quickly overshadow group strengths in areas such as 'capability' or 'self-care'.

If your team is not functioning very well at the moment you will need a multi-level and prioritised plan, focussed on all components.

While each component is addressed separately here, each interrelates in some way. When you focus on optimising resources, (resourceful), for example you will be putting in place planning and problem solving processes that are also useful in aspects of 'perseverance' and 'capability'.

There will also be events in people's personal lives that affect work performance and teamwork. While the book highlights activity at work, some of the R@W components such as 'connected' and 'self-care' consider home factors.

Be strategic in your approach

A strategic approach is recommended as it is unrealistic to invest in all of the components of resilience-building simultaneously. Once your team's strengths and gaps have been identified then work together to prioritise actions.

If your team is under-performing at the moment it is important to identify the components that are having the most impact. As an example, if workload is unrelenting and people are becoming exhausted, attention to being alert to early signs of overload and establishing boundaries (self-care), together with regular re-grouping on priorities (resourceful) may be important. In times of organisational change, collective proactivity (robust) and accessing external support (capability) may be of greater importance.

It's a case of regularly assessing the operational challenges and determining which R@W components are most relevant at that time.

Address the 'elephant in the room'

If there is a significant issue within the team, such as bad behaviour by one or more members, people may be reluctant to engage in broader resilience building without some assurance that this is also being addressed. When there is dysfunction you will need to work on a plan to restore a reasonable level of relationships and communication before you can work collectively on building resilience. This may require getting external specialist assistance.

Review your plan regularly

As outlined in Chapter 1, resilience is a dynamic state, which means that as demands shift or increase you need to review and adapt your strategies. It is not unusual for external factors such as changed funding, or internal factors such as new leadership, to change group dynamics. Attention to *how* a team conducts its work is as important as *what* it does and yet the former generally gets less attention.

Manage up

This book explores actions that are within the scope of the team itself to change. Clearly the impact of these can be inhibited by broader organisational factors. As an example a focus on clear roles and shared direction (robust) within the team is limited by a lack of overall strategic direction. Similarly, the success of optimising resources (resourceful) is affected by the workload expected of the team.

Some of these issues can be addressed through managing up. If your team is struggling on a number of fronts, it is best to manage up strategically. It's rather like managing teenagers as it's a case of choosing which battles to fight. Managing up on all issues can risk your team being seen as problematic.

It is also useful to identify the factors that impact on resilience but are outside of the influence of the team to change. Openly naming these can allow discussion around better managing the impact of these.

Case study – restructuring the resistant team

A community services organisation employed a team of passionate professionals. The group was talented, creative and cohesive. Over a period of two years a number of changes to services were implemented as a result of budget pressures and government policy. Members of the team fought against all of the changes as they believed that they were not in the interest of the community they served. The leader, who had been promoted from within the team, advocated assertively for her team's position when conversing with management. Over time the team were perceived as change resistant. When a major restructure occurred the team was dissolved and its members were assigned to other groups. The manager failed to win a leadership positon.

Be open to new opportunities

Shifts in our environment such as a change in employees, management, processes, funding, structure or customer expectations can often offer new opportunities. The key is to be alert and open to changes in the working environment that the team can capitalise on.

Top Tips

Changes around us can create opportunities for us if we are open to them.

Now that you have a good snapshot of how you see your team's resilience at the moment you can explore each of the seven components more fully through case studies and exercises in the following chapters.

⚙ Top Tips

Value and build on what you have already

We often don't appreciate, or recognise, what we are already doing that is working well for us. Being more conscious about these actions means they are more likely to be valued and kept precious by the team. Building on them is also easier than trying something completely different.

Be clear on the current state of your team's resilience

To develop a plan, you first need to identify where you are now. Recognise though that resilience is dynamic rather than fixed so it may change as your working environment shifts.

Beware the panacea

Be careful not to downplay the challenges inherent in the job. While resilience is essential, it is not the answer to all of the issues a team may be experiencing

Focus where you will have most impact

Think strategically. Where are the main gaps in your resilience toolkit and what changes will have the most impact for the team at the moment? Are there issues that will overshadow others that need attention before people will engage in developing a resilience plan?

Don't make the plan a project that creates more work

The last thing a busy team needs is another project. The most manageable approach is to consider small changes in everyday activities and routines. Each change may seem limited but a number of small shifts on a number of levels can add up to a significant improvement in how you manage the weekly challenges you face.

Extend the team's influence

Be clear what is outside of the influence of your team to change but do not discount the ability to collectively manage up on significant issues. Be alert and open to new opportunities for influencing that may arise through changes in the work environment.

| Chapter 5
 | **Robust**

T1 Robust

Having shared purpose, goals and values and the skills needed to do the job. Being proactive when issues arise for the team.

To be a resilient team we need to be competent in what we are employed to do. We need to have the talent required, as well as agreed purpose, direction and values. We also need to share ownership of issues that arise. These elements are not new and have been long established as important in teamwork. This chapter explores how they relate to resilience.

Creating shared purpose

Generally, people are more resilient if they are emotionally engaged with what they are doing – that is, if they can relate to a purpose and a belief in the activities they are asked to do.

Quick Quip

"When this job ceases to be life giving I'm leaving." (Comment from a team leader managing a difficult team).

If we translate this to groups, it means that teams need to be clear on why they are doing tasks and the values or principles that guide how they do them.

For a team to be resilient, the 'why' and 'how' need to be agreed and shared. A person can be quite clear in their own principles and purpose but if this is in conflict with colleagues it can disrupt teamwork and create dissatisfaction and even turnover. People often leave a job because of a misalignment with personal values and beliefs.

Keeping the 'Why' central

Organisations often work to create a sense of purpose through vision and mission statements. Such initiatives provide a necessary foundation for a group to work from but still require translation at the team level for them to be meaningful. Each team needs to connect what they are doing to why they are doing it.

Case study – flowers for Mother's Day

A university student was on a placement at an aged care facility and was asked to deliver flowers to a resident on Mother's Day. Enthusiastically she took off to the room and carefully arranged them in the corner. Mrs Jones had only peripheral vision and was unable to see them. The card sat unannounced and unopened next to the vase on what was a very special day of the year. The student returned to the supervisor pleased with her efficiency but the purpose and meaning of the task was missed.

Engaging people in the 'why' is easier in jobs where members are contributing to a customer or community service they believe in, rather than making business shareholders richer. Purpose is not always clearly defined though and may shift as circumstances change. For example, reforms in aged and disability care towards client-directed models may colour whether the purpose is support and care or independence.

In organisations where there are conflicting roles for employees, there may also be disparity across teams. For example, the purpose of a workplace safety regulator may be education as well as regulation. Which one becomes a priority depends on the team you are assigned to. Child protection is another good example where teams may be assigned to family reunification or regulation. Conflicts such as these can create confusion within the organisation itself.

Regardless of the organisational context, discussing and defining purpose within a team is a useful activity to undertake. The outcome becomes the lighthouse for activity and the reason why people are willing to work hard.

Quick Quip

"I'm an auditor and my wife is an intensive care nurse." (An accountant reflecting on job purpose).

Sometimes a team's purpose is clear and agreed but a disconnection arises through an inability to fulfil it. A common example is when budget cuts impact on the quality or quantity of outcomes a team can achieve. People often describe this as a loss of integrity in the work, or an incapacity to maintain reasonable levels of professionalism. Teams voicing such concerns are more likely to see their work as a vocation. They are generally employed in not-for-profit roles, public service jobs or work that has clear company values or professional practice standards.

In other situations, strong risk aversion within a team or organisation may mean that purpose becomes lost in processes that take the energy away from delivering the service.

If the reason why a team performs a role is compromised it can cause disengagement and have a detrimental impact on resilience.

Quick Quip

"The other day I had to write a brief of a brief. I struggle with how my work adds any value (to our clients) at the end of the day."

Top Tips

Complex work activity can sometimes create a focus on process to the detriment of purpose.

To embed the 'why' within your team ensure that you engage in regular conversations on how the daily tasks connect to the overall purpose. A simple example is discussing how decisions being made within the team will impact on the client, environment, child, patient or community you serve. This focus needs to be at the centre of the discussion, and the guiding principle for decision-making, rather than an after-thought.

Case study – keeping purpose central

A senior health leadership team held a meeting to identify the strategic risks for the service. After three hours the group was happy with the comprehensive list and with the agreed next steps to manage these. As a closing comment one person pointed out that none of the risks they had identified mentioned the patient. A manager quickly added, "Don't worry, they are all about the patient ultimately, we just need to re-write the list to reflect that."

Exercise – Shared purpose

Questions	Reflections
Who or what does your team exist to serve?	
How can team member roles and activities be better aligned to purpose?	

Purpose outside of work

It would be naïve to believe that all jobs offer a purpose. Many people have limited choice around what they do for a living and work to make a living. For some organisations the purpose is simply to make a profit for shareholders. In the latter case organisations are looking to create ways in which the organisation can add value in different ways through volunteering programs, community initiatives or other endeavours that come under the 'corporate responsibility program' banner.

When purpose is missing on a personal level, it is worthwhile finding out of work pursuits that help you feel that your life has meaning and that you are contributing in some way.

Quick Quip

"I have given up believing I can make a difference in my job but have adopted a child from a disadvantaged background. I work for this and so have renewed direction in my life."

Creating shared values

In addition to purpose, it is important that teams feel they are able to work in a way that is consistent with their core values and principles.

Private organisations frequently invest a considerable amount of time and money into establishing and promoting their corporate values. It is considered necessary for establishing the business brand, as well as defining the organisational culture. Not-for-profit organisations can look to align behaviours with altruistic principles, while religious bodies seek consistency with their overarching faith. Government bodies use codes of conduct and values consistent with what the public expect of services.

The success of this depends largely on how well the values are translated into the behaviours of the leaders and staff employed. Stated values are not the same as lived values. A perceived disconnect, especially by senior leaders, can create more cynicism and disengagement than anything else. If transparency is the articulated corporate value but there is little sharing of information, for example, what is role modelled always wins over what is espoused.

At a group level, it is important to discuss how the corporate values translate into team activities. A value of 'support' in one team, as an example, may include staff providing practical back-up on daily tasks, while for others it may mean having disagreements in private and ensuring a united front in public. A value of 'courage' may mean offering leading edge solutions in the design team but speaking up without being judged in the risk management team.

It is sometimes useful to develop a team charter or similar document that outlines the expectations team members have of each other. This ensures clarity of how the values translate into action on the ground. It becomes a written version of 'how we do things around here'. This tends to be different from codes of conduct as the latter tend to focus on core professional behaviours that are important to all organisations such as respect and honesty. Mostly, charters become a blend of the translation of organisational values and the code of conduct if, that is, an organisation has both.

Charters are best written in an aspirational way - phrased so that they state what the team wants rather than what it doesn't want. If a lot of undesirable behaviours are occurring, it may be useful though to have a separate list that outlines what is not acceptable. Sometimes these need to be made explicit, especially when they have become part of everyday behaviours.

Trust and respect can be the first aspects to disappear when there is stress and conflict and are the most difficult to restore. Malicious gossip can increase and even common courtesies such as greetings can fall away. Interestingly, this can still happen when people have excellent interpersonal skills, especially when work is high in emotional labour. It seems that acting professionally with clients or customers all day means there is less energy and tolerance to engage professionally with colleagues. There is also an expectation that colleagues should understand the pressures and be more accepting of bad behaviour. Unfortunately, this does not lend to a respectful work environment.

Working directly on respect and trust is difficult but exploring and holding to the agreed team actions that create these is easier. In terms of overall resilience, this is a critical starting point. If respectful communication is missing other aspects of teamwork such as problem solving, capability building and workload management are difficult to achieve.

Quick Quip

"The atmosphere in the team is toxic. One person wears sunglasses to meetings and looks the other way when I am speaking."

A charter needs to be a live document, rather than something placed on the intranet or on the office or lunchroom wall. It can be integrated into selection and induction processes, service agreements, project set-ups, planning processes and referred to regularly at team meetings and in general communication. Integrated in this way, at the team level, it can be a very powerful way to embed desired behaviours.

Case study – values box

Staff at a community centre developed a team charter and decided to focus on one aspect per month. They set up a feedback box so that staff and customers could write thank you notes to people they saw demonstrate that value during the month. Each month they opened the box together and shared the notes at their staff meeting. It became a way of expressing gratitude to each other as well as a reminder to align thoughts and actions with values.

Clearly articulated expectations are especially valuable in preventing the occurrence of poor behaviour if they are introduced at induction and regularly monitored and discussed by the team. It is always helpful for managers to be able to refer to expectations that have been generated by the team themselves rather than by leadership. It is also important for colleagues to feel empowered to constructively 'call behaviour' when it is not aligned with what has been agreed.

Quick Quip

"I engaged an external person to develop a team charter for my team. That way when I need to pull up poor behaviour I can refer to the team's expectations, not my own." (Team leader).

Case study – re-visiting team values

A small professional team was working in a role where there was ample opportunity to showcase outcomes through presentations and public reports. The team worked collaboratively and harmoniously in a complex and challenging environment. Each person felt equally valued despite the different levels of seniority and the team's work was widely regarded as high in quality.

A senior member joined with a very different way of working and interpersonal relationships quickly broke down.

Given the ensuing disharmony, the team decided to re-group to define the culture that they wanted to create and the expectations they had of each other in creating this.

What became evident from the discussion was that important values that the team had taken for granted were being breached. Their core values were, in their words, 'sharing the glory and stretch' and 'we are all equal'.

The new colleague, while highly talented, had been seizing on any opportunity he could for himself, asserting his seniority over more junior members and attempting to take credit for the unit's work.

Clearly defining team member expectations allowed the team to restore harmony. It was also important to define concrete examples of the values important to them. For example, 'sharing the glory' included a requirement for written and verbal acknowledgements of co-workers at presentations and in reports. Aspects of 'sharing the stretch' involved the group deciding together who would take on interesting assignments and 'we are all equal' involved members not automatically assigning basic tasks to team members with less seniority.

Top Tips

Establishing and monitoring expectations during induction is an effective way of ensuring values alignment from the outset.

Exercise – Shared team values

Questions	Reflections
What are your team's lived values?	
How are the values communicated and shared?	

Questions	Reflections
Would it be useful to develop a team charter and how would you make it a living document?	
How can you improve the way in which team members positively 'call behaviour' when it breaches agreed values?	

More on interpersonal communication, as it relates to resilience is explored in the chapters on the R@W Team components of 'connected' and 'alignment'.

Developing shared goals

Once purpose and values are agreed, the task is then to determine work goals.

Our individual goals and tasks are often well defined through job descriptions and performance indicators or benchmarks. The important factor when we are considering team resilience however is whether these goals are shared and aligned. A work climate where there is competition between colleagues, high criticism, silos, fixed roles or differing perceived responsibilities may work counter to this.

We know that interdependence of team member activities enhances a sense of shared goals but can also be the source of conflict or dissatisfaction. It's a bit like the group project at university when someone can end up doing most of the work to ensure a high grade and becomes resentful at the lack of contribution from others.

The essential resilience aspect is mutual accountability and flexibility for work output and goals. These aspects are explored later in the chapters on 'alignment' and 'connected'.

When operating environments are turbulent, goals may need frequent re-visiting and re-allocation. The concept of an annual planning cycle is under threat in many industries due to uncertainty and unexpected change. This need for regularly revisiting priorities and work allocation is part of the 'resourceful' aspect of the R@W Team discussed in the next chapter.

Quick Quip

"We used to do five-year planning then three-year. Now we are lucky if the plan stays valid for 12 months as there is so much happening."

Having the talent required

Without the skill and knowledge required to get the work done, no amount of shared purpose, values and direction is going to ensure a team performs. It's a bit like a rugby team without players able to run, kick and scrum. A team needs to have members with the talent required.

The easiest approach to this is to recruit the talent you need. This may not always be possible as there may be skill shortages, or you may be finding it difficult to source skilled staff who have values aligned with your organisation.

Talent management within organisations is an extensive topic outside of the scope of this book. It can include, amongst other activities, professional development, 360-degree and other feedback mechanisms, assessment centres, mentoring, coaching and fast tracking of high performers. The focus in this book is on activities that can be implemented by the team itself, without necessarily needing organisational programs or support, although the latter is always preferable.

Within Chapter 9 we focus on building our talent pool through connecting to external resources and in Chapter 11 we explore maximising the use of existing skills and experience.

Being proactive around issues

The final aspect of the 'robust' component relates to how teams respond to problems that arise.

One of the interesting aspects around building resilience within teams is that members will often be reluctant to engage in positive activities and directions when there is an unresolved issue that is seen as problematic. People can be unwilling to adopt a strengths and growth approach when challenges have been neither acknowledged nor addressed. As detailed in the section on values above, unresolved interpersonal conflict or lack of respect are good examples of this.

In developing your team plan identifying and naming the so-called 'elephants in the room' is critical and often the starting point for restoring resilience. Not only can these be a blockage to people engaging in important activities, they can also have a detrimental impact and erode the level of resilience that exists.

Case study – elephant in the room

The team was expanding. There was additional funding for staff, new offices opening and promotional opportunities. Feedback from customers was excellent and members enjoyed an enviable reputation within their sector.

Despite the outward indicators being positive, morale within the team was low. Members were excited about growth but did not want the existing tension and issues to taint the new staff coming in.

At the heart of the issue was a manager who the team liked and felt loyalty towards. While he had been the right person when the service was small, his team knew that he did not have what was needed to take the service to the next level. The manager himself was not open to feedback around his limitations. A couple of members had vocalised their concerns to the Human Resources Department but the majority felt torn in their allegiances.

An external facilitator was brought in to assist in resolving the leadership issue. Without doing this the staff were unable to fully embrace the opportunities ahead.

There are a variety of issues that can occur in a team and some of the common ones are covered throughout the book. What is important to emphasise here is the need for teams to take responsibility for addressing these constructively and collectively as they arise, and before they either block growth or impact negatively on existing performance. To be a robust team there needs to be shared attention to early problem resolution.

⚙ Top Tips

Keep the 'why' central in what you do

Be clear about why your team exists and link work activity and decision-making to this. People are more engaged and motivated if they understand how their job contributes to something they believe in. If your work has purpose it becomes more of a vocation than a job.

Use shared values to guide how you operate

Discuss what team members expect of each other. Write this up in a charter. Review it regularly and hold each other to what is agreed. That way team values will become lived, rather than a document on a wall or shared computer drive.

Align goals

While some degree of competition can be healthy, ensure that members contribute to shared team goals, and not just their own. Create a sense of 'we're all in this together.'

Recruit and develop the talent you need

Develop team member capabilities in line with shifting demands. Put in place mechanisms to review and build the skills and knowledge required to work optimally.

Resolve issues promptly

Promote joint responsibility for resolving team issues, rather than relying on management.

| Chapter 6

⊕ | **Resourceful**

T2 Resourceful

Harnessing team member strengths and resources and building a culture of continuous improvement.

Developing effective team processes that enable a clear focus on priorities.

The need for teams to optimise the resources they have has become of greater importance as budgets and staff numbers decline, concurrent with job demands staying constant or increasing. Often there is more to do than there is capacity to do. As a result, a new aspect of team effectiveness involves developing ways to capitalise on what you have, as well as processes to re-prioritise. Added to this is a need to continually adapt to changing expectations around what the team does. In summary, teams need to be resourceful.

Establishing processes to optimise resources

If your workplace has an unpredictable workload such as ad hoc requests or large variability in service demands, you may need to establish a process to jointly determine how to optimise resources, if this is not already established.

While we each have to be accountable for our own time and workload management, having group approaches ensures that activities are aligned around unit priorities. Without this, teams can easily get pulled into tasks that are urgent but not necessarily important. In the worst case scenario, it can develop into daily crisis management with no strategic approach around how the team operates.

What a team process looks like will vary significantly between teams. In some, it may require a 5-minute morning check-in. For others, it could be a weekly regroup to reconsider priorities, or a periodic review of plans. The more turbulent the working environment, the more frequent the re-group mechanism needs to be.

Quick Quip

"Everything here is urgent. We now have to ask if it's urgent-urgent."

Managing under-performing resources

Generally, the most important resource in a team is its members. As staffing numbers become leaner we all need to contribute 100 per cent effort most of the time. The capacity to buffer lack of effort is less possible and can cause resentment. When we are stressed with our own workload, covering for others is not looked upon favourably. As a result, managing under-performance becomes more critical. It is another example of the need to maximise use of the available resources.

Sharing physical resources

As well as optimising our use of human capital, it is important to share physical resources such as equipment and office space. Agile working is a good example of maximising use of the latter. Perceived ownership, or competition for resources are the biggest obstacles to sharing.

Top Tips

You need to be clear on what resources you already have before determining how to maximise their use.

Case study – pooling resources

Madge was the manager of a child-care centre. The staff frequently complained that they did not have enough educational and play equipment but there was limited budget to purchase more. After-hours one evening Madge asked the staff to bring all of the resources into one room. She facilitated a discussion on how they could better use what they owned. What became obvious was the under-utilisation of what was in the pile in front of them and how perceived ownership of resources was preventing better use. Most of the resources were kept in the respective rooms and were seen as 'belonging' to that room and that team.

Capitalising on team member strengths

Another way in which we can optimise the resources we have is through capitalising on the strengths of our team members.

When we talk about strengths within a work setting we are referring not only to skills and knowledge, but also personal strengths that can assist performance such as creativity, critical thinking and relationship building.

In recent years, considerable research has been done into the concept of personal or character strengths. This emerges from what is known as positive psychology – a branch of psychology that explores how we might live a flourishing life.

The research indicates that working in alignment with our strengths promotes our personal well-being, as well as our sense of engagement in our work.

The theory is that we are most likely to grow and thrive in our areas of strength and that it is better to identify and capitalise on these rather than engage in aspects that we are less competent in.

The first step is to identify what strengths members hold and how these can be used to better advantage by the group. The second step is to enable use of these through modifying roles or removing obstacles that stop people deploying them. You could also look at ways to build on, and develop, strengths through identifying opportunities such as projects or assignments. This is known in the trade as 'job crafting'.

Using staff strengths to full advantage, in alignment with team goals, is a smart way to optimise the people resources within your group.

Case study – using strengths post downsizing

A work unit of 80 people in a financial services unit underwent a budget cut that resulted in 17 voluntary redundancies. Many of those who chose to leave were late in their career and held substantial corporate knowledge and technical skill. Those who were left were allocated to new teams.

Morale was low and there was considerable concern that the loss of staff would mean there was not enough senior people left who could provide the advice and technical support needed.

The division regrouped to identify the strengths of those still employed and how these could be better used both within and across teams. Previously, teams had limited mechanisms to mentor, train and support each other across units.

The outcome was greater confidence in the talent that remained and strategies to use and tap into this.

Top Tips

We need to know the strengths of our team members to capitalise on them.

Exercise – Optimising resources

Questions	Reflections
What processes do you use in your team to ensure you are working in-line with changing priorities?	
How are physical resources pooled for maximum advantage?	

Questions	Reflections
How could you better harness the strengths of team members?	

Establishing a climate of continuous improvement

Resilient teams not only adapt to change they also drive it. They regularly look for opportunities to improve the way in which they deliver outcomes.

To be adaptable, teams needs to be alert to changes in the environment that may impact on them. They engage routinely in what is known in strategic planning as 'environmental scanning'. A key enabler for this is good external networks. These could be within the organisation, for example access to others who understand the vision of a newly appointed director. It could also mean being well connected outside of the organisation. It may be useful, for example, to have access to people who are conversant with emerging trends in better practice or well informed about political, financial, community or other factors relevant to the team.

Creating a climate of continuous improvement also requires members to be willing to openly share, listen to and critique ideas. This means competence in engaging in constructive disagreement. Adaptable teams work through conflicting views without a negative impact on relationships. Within them, people can challenge the status quo and generate new ideas without concern that anyone will feel threatened.

Quick Quip

"Our principle is 'play the ball, not the person'. We have heated debates but we don't take it personally and leave the disagreement behind us in the room."

Case study – continuous improvement in orthopaedics

Surgical units sometimes have a reputation for being hierarchical, with an unwritten culture of not questioning the judgement of senior surgeons. This can run counter to continuous improvement and patient safety as it inhibits communication and the perceived ability of more junior staff to question practices or raise concerns.

An orthopaedic department in a large teaching hospital developed a culture of continuous improvement through:

- Developing meeting structures that created space for junior staff to contribute
- Joint responsibility for researching and benchmarking practice within the unit
- Capacity for non-judgmental discussion on concerns and mistakes
- Accessibility to senior clinicians
- A supportive, rather than judgmental, leadership style
- Equity of input, with the opinions of all professionals and support staff valued.

Being adaptable to change

Implicit in developing an environment that values continuous improvement is a positive attitude towards change.

The language around change can sometimes be quite negative. We talk about change fatigue, change resistance and how change can be a journey similar to the stages of grief.

Models of change that propose a start and end point are becoming less relevant as often there are a number of transitions happening simultaneously. In these circumstances it may be better to talk about being nimble, adaptable and flexible, rather than focusing on how best to manage and move through yet another change.

Top Tips

Try talking about adaptability rather than change management.

Case study - resistance or change readiness?

A team of workers had been sheltered from the impact of major changes in their organisation because of their specialised skill and role. Work activity was highly structured and many of the team had worked in the unit for many years – largely doing the same role. Interaction outside of the team was predominantly seen as the manager's job.

When the team were required to move location, this alone resulted in a couple of people resigning. They did not react well to the prospect of the change. Some people labelled them as 'change resistant'.

Is this a reasonable criticism, given they had worked in a very stable environment with limited need for adaptability?

Top Tips

The more a team embeds mechanisms for adaptability into how they work the easier it is to respond to imposed change.

Exercise – Adaptability

Questions	Reflections
How in-tune is your team with outside influences it may need to respond to?	
How can you better develop an environment that values continuous improvement?	

Questions	Reflections
What can you do to ensure members can safely challenge the status quo?	

"If it ain't broke, don't fix it." (A businessman overheard commenting on quotas for the number of women on Boards).

Effectively managing workload

The final element of the 'resourceful' component relates to teams effectively managing the workload together. Elements explored here are clarity of responsibilities, mutual accountability and managing the expectations of leadership.

Establishing clear responsibilities and mutual accountability

Resilient teams combine clarity of individual responsibilities with mutual accountability for achieving the overall goals of the team.

Clear responsibilities

A key criterion for effective workload management is defining roles and responsibilities. However, while individuals need to understand what their duties are, a degree of flexibility is necessary for collective outcomes.

Fixed roles may be an obstacle in this. Detailed job descriptions or rigid professional boundaries can sometimes work against collaboration. In environments where activities are often shifting, aligning people with the functions needed to create outcomes is far more beneficial that detailed task lists. In some situations, members may use these documents to maintain rigid role boundaries, and so ultimately work against team effort.

Quick Quip

"Why should I help? – That's not my job."

Mutual accountability

Effective teams understand and enforce the notion of mutual accountability. They understand that they need to perform their own tasks, but also contribute to the team's overall goals. One way this can be reinforced is by tracking, and communicating, both individual and team progress.

Tracking individual output is best achieved through regular private manager meetings with each person. While this may be obvious, one-to-one meetings have fallen off in frequency in many workplaces – another casualty of the general 'busyness' of jobs. Interestingly, when team performance goes off-track, restoring such meetings is one of the first things recommended to leaders. Preserving time for these is therefore a good preventative measure.

To build a culture of mutual responsibility it is useful for team members to be held accountable for joint as well as personal performance. This is in contrast to creating competitiveness between individuals that may run counter to group performance. Visual tracking of team member responsibilities against overall goals is always useful for this – whether this is a simple spread sheet, graphic or a plan on a whiteboard or shared drive. This needs to be sensitively balanced with confidential discussions around individual poor performance.

Case study – mutual accountability

Staff in the supermarket would often blame the previous shift for tasks not done. In the main, these were activities such as cleaning that were everyone's responsibility rather than the role of one person. To add to the confusion, managers from other areas would directly observe issues on the floor but would say nothing. They did not want to tread on the toes of fellow managers.

To resolve the situation, the managers agreed on what problems should be tackled directly when observed, and which issues should be referred back to each other to deal with. Within the respective teams, staff drew up a list of the shared tasks and principles were agreed on how these should be actioned.

In this way both the managers and staff participated in developing mutual accountability for tasks that did not clearly fit within any one person's job description.

Quick Quip

"I'm not your mother." (a note left in a messy staff kitchen).

Top Tips

Mutual accountability does not happen by chance. It needs clear expectations, and sometimes team structures, around equity of effort.

Motivation and mutual accountability

When discussing mutual accountability, it is useful to explore the impact of personal motivation. Our accountability is driven by whether we 'want to', 'have to' or 'ought to' engage in activities that contribute to team goals.

'Want to'

Instilling a 'want to' attitude is the best way to motivate us as this means we will have an emotional commitment to action. Connecting work to a shared team purpose is one important way to instil emotional commitment. Engaging people in tasks that use their strengths is another. Positive energy and enthusiasm around us also helps, as does planning and making decisions together.

'Have to'

The 'have to' element drives us when the costs of not doing something outweigh the costs of doing it. It's the punishment part of the 'carrot and the stick' aspect of motivation. Tracking our contribution towards team progress and individual performance, conversations fall into the 'have to' category. When emotional commitment is high, there is less need for this conditional type of motivation.

'Ought to'

The final aspect of motivation, 'ought to', occurs when we feel a moral obligation to do something. Within the workplace this tends to include aspects such as personal conscientiousness and professionalism, as well as perceived peer pressure or concerns about reputation and maintaining relationships that are important to us.

Strategies that leverage from all three of these motivation drivers, in appropriate measures, can instil mutual accountability.

Case study – the minimalist worker

Colleagues described Rosemary as a dominating character who was fond of telling everyone else what to do but made little contribution herself. She didn't seem to be concerned at the impact this had on others. Those who had worked with her over a long period had become used to it and were reluctant to challenge her, as the upset it caused when she reacted to feedback wasn't worth the effort. Typically, her response to criticism was to ignore people and to do even less than normal for several days.

Rosemary's colleagues felt that it was the team leader's job to address her poor work ethic and disrespect, but with a lack of response from that direction their usual response was to finish off her outstanding tasks.

The team took on two new team members from another department who noticed that their colleagues were letting Rosemary get away with minimal output. They decided that if she could get away with it so could they and they acted accordingly.

Rosemary had neither the 'want to' nor 'ought to' components of motivation and with an absence of 'have to' (from the team as well as the leader), she limited the degree of mutual accountability needed.

Top Tips

Not addressing a lack of accountability from one person can create a work environment where this becomes acceptable.

Misguided interpretations of poor performance

Occasionally, managers fall into the trap of assuming that poor performance is due to a lack of motivation rather than a lack of capacity. The reality is that if a person is not capable of the work, physically or intellectually, no amount of support or pressure will significantly change that.

In organisations where staff have been employed a long time and job demands are shifting this can become an issue. An administrative worker who was employed when the job involved greeting and directing people at reception, for example, may not have the intellect or aptitude to move to complex administrative tasks.

Case study – when the role outgrows the person

William had worked in the organisation for 30 years and was almost an institution. Everyone liked him. He worked in the mailroom sorting incoming and outgoing mail and did that successfully and independently. With the advent of email, the amount of written communication decreased to the extent that this role took up less and less time and other basic administrative duties were assigned to him.

William was eventually assigned to a service support team and given considerable training in his new duties. Despite this support there were complaints from colleagues about his motivation and the quality and quantity of his work. They started to do the work themselves rather than give it to him to perform.

William remained his usual upbeat and friendly self and pretended to be managing, even though he wasn't. He was worried that there was no other role for him and that he may be made redundant.

A new manager in her first leadership role was assigned to the team. She decided to give William more interesting tasks in order to try to motivate him. This simply compounded the problem, as the new duties were all far too much of a stretch. The team leader started to question her competence as a leader – feeling that she had failed both William and the team.

The reality was that William did not have the level of intelligence to do the new role and no amount of training and support could change this.

Top Tips

Consider whether it's a 'will do' or 'can do' factor when accountability for performance appears to be missing.

Exercise – Instilling mutual accountability

Questions	Reflections
How is mutual accountability for outcomes established, communicated and tracked? What could you do better?	

Questions	Reflections
How is a lack of accountability for performance managed by your team? What could you do better?	

Managing leader expectations of workload

In some situations, teams may believe that the real issue is unrealistic expectations from senior leadership. If this is the case, the task of the team becomes one of managing up. This needs to be done sensitively, balancing a willingness to achieve targets with expression of concerns about what is viable.

Top Tips

Managing up can be like parenting teenagers. You need to choose your battles to win the war.

Case study – managing expectations around workload

A group of professionals were becoming concerned that constant budget cuts were affecting their capacity to maintain what they considered were acceptable levels of professional practice. They were a hardworking group who had chosen to accommodate a series of changes and just get on with what they were asked to do. This was despite having real concerns.

Some months earlier they had seen a group in another division disappear after a restructure. That team had been very vocal on all aspects of the changes and had fought each one. As a consequence, management had labelled them a problem.

This team were unhappy with a multitude of factors and felt strongly that they could not continue with further erosion of service standards. Mindful of the fate of the team that was disbanded, they decided to be strategic and chose two of the changes that were especially problematic for them. They developed a plan to influence senior leadership in both of these areas. Developing the plan, in itself, was motivating as the team felt they were more empowered to restore aspects of the job that had been eroded. The plan was well received.

⚙ Top Tips

Make the best use of what you have

Regularly review priorities and workload allocation to ensure resources are being used in an optimal way. Know the strengths of team members and leverage from them. It is more productive, and satisfying, to work with tasks we are naturally good at.

Build mutual accountability

Put in place processes that track work activity in a way that establishes mutual accountability for outcomes. Minimise competition or inequities that work against shared responsibility.

Manage the 'minimalist' performers

Recognise that when we need to perform at full capacity the majority of the time to get our work done, we can be reluctant to carry others. A lack of attention to members not pulling their weight can create resentment. It also inhibits optimising the resources we have available.

Optimise the motivators

Encourage the 'want to', 'have to' and 'ought to' drivers for teamwork. If we want to do something, if there are consequences for not doing it, and if we feel a moral obligation towards doing it, we have captured all three drivers.

Promote adaptability

Challenge negative communication or mindsets around change. Focus on developing flexibility rather than presenting change as something to be managed or resisted. Build processes that provide space for the team to review and improve the way the job is done. This creates a culture of continuous improvement and makes imposed change easier.

Manage workload expectations

Unrealistic expectations about what a team can do may need a 'managing up' approach. Work on a strategic influencing plan to get the facts heard and appreciated.

| Chapter 7

 | **Perseverance**

T3 Perseverance

Staying optimistic and having a solution, rather than a problem, focus.

Persisting in the face of obstacles.

When the working week is difficult, and regularly paved with obstacles, persisting and remaining optimistic is a challenge. To be resilient a team needs perseverance.

Engendering optimism

The word, 'optimism' is often interchanged with the word 'resilience', possibly because it is hard to have one without the other.

Optimistic teams respond to setbacks and good news in a different manner to those with a more pessimistic outlook. When things go wrong they are less inclined to blame themselves unnecessarily and they see the event as a temporary setback. They also compartmentalise the incident and do not let it pervade other things that are happening. Alternatively, when a positive event happens they see that they have contributed to it, consider it as lasting and let it flow on to the rest of their work and life.

Reviewing the examples below, which of these responses best reflects how your team would respond to both a setback and success?

Example – Optimistic versus pessimistic viewpoints

After a setback	Pessimistic responses	Optimistic responses
Personalising a setback	'We should never have got them involved in this. Now it's a disaster.'	'Getting them involved didn't work for us. What have we learned from this that we can use next time?'
Seeing a set-back as permanent	'That's the last shot we had at making that work.'	'What are our options from here? How do we resurrect this and give it another go?'
Letting a set-back pervade other aspects of work	'There's no point going out for a drink together. We have nothing to celebrate.'	'Let's go for a drink and celebrate how well we've stuck together through this.'

After a success	Pessimistic responses	Optimistic responses
Not taking the credit for success	'We were lucky that it worked.'	'We put in a lot of effort into making that work.'
Seeing a success as temporary	'We might have had a win this time but we are still likely to fail overall.'	'This (success) demonstrates that we are good at this.'
Not letting the success affect other aspects of the team's work	'That might have worked this time but everything else is a struggle.'	'This win is certainly going to lift our spirits and make us more energised to take on all our other problems.'

The overall level of optimism within a team is, of course, variable and contingent on how members respond to incidents. While we cannot always directly shift a colleague's pessimism we can influence and raise the level of optimism within the team through being mindful of the way in which we talk about both setbacks and successes. We need to make sure it is realistic though. Blind optimism that does not consider the reality and the risks is highly problematic, especially if you are in a leadership position.

Team leader optimism

As a team leader you cannot afford to be pessimistic, as this will have a negative impact on your staff. At the same time, you cannot be too positive, as unrealistic optimism will quickly alienate others. Your team may conclude that you are out of touch with the real issues and may worry that you do not appreciate what their job entails.

Unfortunately, managers are occasionally unaware of this as they are recruited on the basis of an ambitious vision for a team without knowing that it is not aligned with the reality on the ground.

Generating the right balance of remaining upbeat while being realistic about the challenges you face can be hard work. This is especially the case when you have to translate unpopular messages from managers above you in a way that maintains some degree of motivation within your team.

To maintain your personal optimism, create a safe place where you can privately discuss your concerns, voice your negativity and gain ideas and perspective. Without this space it may be difficult to maintain the optimism you need to display.

Case study – leadership optimism

On the announcement of an organisational merger many of the front-line managers voiced negative opinions to their staff. Some saw the merger as an unwelcome take-over, while others were quite content working in a smaller entity. A few simply believed that the restructure would not work. All of them knew, however, that half of the management positions would be lost.

What those who were being openly pessimistic did not consider, was how they were going to restore optimism with their staff, post-restructure. Bringing staff through the change was going to be even more difficult for managers who openly criticised it.

Top Tips

Demonstrating optimism even when you feel pessimistic is an integral part of sound team leadership.

Creating positive energy

Closely linked to optimism is the creation of positive energy within our teams. Without it problems become even more overwhelming and we struggle to stay motivated.

Psychology researchers have demonstrated that emotion is contagious. It seems that we can catch and feel the emotions around us. This means that when we engender positivity within our teams it builds on itself. The flow-on benefit is that our relationships and productivity improve and we are more open to exploring solutions and developing creative options.

Case study - emotional contagion

The team leader was an unusual character with a negative aura that inhibited others from approaching her. She also rarely had anything positive to say.

The atmosphere within the cramped office area was tense and all three team members had physical symptoms that they attributed to working all day in the negative energy. One had migraines, one experienced back problems and one was suffering recurrence of a skin disorder. They all enjoyed the job but the tension within the office was physically and psychologically debilitating.

Top Tips

Negativity around you all day can make you sick.

If your work is emotionally gruelling, such as working with angry people or dealing with complaints all day, it is even more important to balance the negativity of the role with positive energy. While we need people out of work to boost our mood we also need positive energy from our team. One obvious way to do this is through humour.

The power of laughter

Providing opportunities to lighten up and have fun at work helps to cement team relationships and build resilience.

Unfortunately, as jobs become more demanding we have to make more of a conscious effort to have fun and view the lighter side of problems. Spontaneous fun is less likely when we are stressed and grumpy.

Humour is a cheap yet great de-fuser when the pressure is on. It is one of the reasons why in-house black humour is used in jobs where people are frequently exposed to trauma, such as police, ambulance officers and emergency services. People in these roles recognise that it would be highly insensitive to share such humour outside of the group, but find it an effective way to process traumatic events together.

Quick Quip

"We joke a lot in the truck after major incidents. It helps us cope with the trauma of it all but we certainly wouldn't do this outside of our team." (Fire fighter).

Care needs to be taken to make sure that any humour used to manage gruelling situations does not become part of the regular dialogue about clients.

Quick Quip

"We had to pull back on our black humour as it was starting to become too disrespectful of our clients." (Social worker).

Even in work that is not inherently emotionally draining, humour can quickly change or lift the mood. Many of us have a colleague who has that knack of breaking the tension with the right retort at the right moment.

Managing negativity within a team

If emotion is contagious, we need to both enhance positivity and manage negativity. Containing the negativity of selective team members can sometimes be a challenge. In fact, people often comment that one of the most difficult aspects of being on a team can be working with negative or cynical colleagues. Those people always have a reason why something will fail and remind you frequently of past mistakes. They can be de-energising and de-motivating.

When morale is low these people tend to have more influence and become more successful in pulling others towards their dim view of the world.

Be sure to differentiate between negative people and those who provide sound critique. Every team needs someone who challenges decisions and questions whether all risks have been duly considered.

Quick Quip

"Oh, you mean dementers*. We've got one of them. They suck the soul out of you." (*A reference to Harry Potter).

In containing others' negativity, it is generally better to focus on decreasing the airtime given to them rather than wasting energy on changing their outlook. A simple way to do this is to agree in principle with what they are saying, offer a different perspective and then politely turn or walk away.

Here are two examples:

Comment 1: "Management have no idea how much work is involved in making these changes."

Response 1: "Yes, it's certainly a lot of extra effort but it's going to be great for the customers once it's in place."

Comment 2: "This extra workload is totally unrealistic."

Response 2: "You are right; we've got a lot on but we do seem to be able to pull together to get it done."

Note that the aim is not to change the person's viewpoint, as this may be beyond rescue. Instead you neither foster nor take on their negativity. If this approach is used by all of the negative person's colleagues it can make a big difference to the overall impact they have on the team.

Exercise – Creating positive energy

Questions	Reflections
How is positive energy and optimism generated in your team?	
What do you do to lighten up and have fun within your team?	

Savouring positive events

Another useful way of engendering positivity is savouring the good events that happen.

To illustrate, let's relate savouring to a scenario where one of your colleagues has come back from a training course excited and wanting to share what was covered and how the team could apply it. How you could respond is listed in the example below.

Example – Responses to a positive event

Dismissive response: "I did the course too. It's okay in theory but it doesn't work around here."

Uninterested response: "Yes, it's great to get a day off from being at work isn't it?"

Passive positive response: "Glad you liked it, I enjoyed it too."

Savouring response: "Tell me more. What did you find the most useful; what did you think of XYX; who else was there that you enjoyed meeting; how do you think we could put the ideas into action?"

The dismissive and uninterested responses are obvious deflators for the excited colleague. The passive positive response does not capitalise on the opportunity to enjoy the positive event. However, just spending five minutes sharing and savouring what happened during the training course can make a significant difference to the overall energy of both parties. If savouring is the usual response to good news in a team it can make a big difference to the overall level of positivity. Taking the time to engage in this way is a significant investment in relationships and resilience.

The R@W component of 'perseverance' is not only about having the optimism and energy to take on challenges, it also requires collective problem solving.

Effective problem solving and decision-making

Effective problem solving processes within a team provide the channel for translating optimism into decisions and actions.

Resilient teams try to focus their energy on where they can make a difference and ensure that they work together on potential solutions to the problems they encounter.

Focusing energy on where it can make a difference

When morale is low, for example during times of unpopular change, it is not uncommon for teams to start to spend more time in the 'isn't it awful conversations' – the type of communication we have when we want to share concerns, disappointment or even anger. It could be that these conversations begin to dominate meetings, or that concerns take up significant airtime in coffee shop or lunchtime catch-ups.

Sharing our feelings and concerns is useful initially as it allows us to vent and get things off our chest, but if it continues it can become quite immobilising. You can find that considerable energy is being expended for no gain. Ultimately, it could create a situation where people take on a victim mentality, believing that they have no influence or control at all. This perceived lack of influence can work against any sense of optimism, engagement or hope.

The first principle in this situation is to be clear about what the team can influence and what it cannot. Members then need to redirect their energy towards what they are able to action and let go of issues they have no control over.

Resilient teams work hard to focus on what they can do rather than spend time worrying about issues outside of their influence. The approach can range from a simple reframe such as 'adapting is what we do' through to a planning exercise that could involve developing a stakeholder influencing plan or actions to manage up.

Quick Quip

"The management team meets weekly and there are always unexpected events that impact on our plans and activities. After about five minutes of venting one of us says 'It is what it is' and that's our cue to stop complaining and get into problem solving mode."

Case study – letting go of what you cannot control

A team of park rangers were working on a number of environmental projects. Major cuts in funding resulted in many of the activities being put on hold or being dropped altogether. This had a major impact on team morale, as there was shared passion around protecting the environment and a deep emotional commitment to the job.

Following the budget cut announcement, the team were upset and angry. For weeks productivity was low as they shared frustrations and were scathing about the projects they were now being asked to implement. The team had become immobilised as they felt they no longer added any real value.

One day at a team meeting, someone suggested that they choose the least objectionable projects and just get on with them. They all agreed and gradually motivation was restored.

The project situation remained unchanged. What had changed was acceptance of the reality and a shift in the direction of their energy and effort.

Quick Quip

"God, grant me the serenity to accept the things I cannot change, courage to change the things I can, and wisdom to know the difference." (The Serenity Prayer).

Exercise – Focusing energy on where you can make a difference

Questions	Reflections
How does your team respond to issues or changes that are outside of its influence or control?	
What, if anything, is your team stuck on that it needs to let go of as it is consuming unnecessary energy?	

Quick Quip

"Problems are us. Without them we don't have a job." (A manager's response to frequent complaints about problems).

Top Tips

Sometimes you have to let go of something to make space for something else to happen.

Deciding which problems are within your influence to address is one aspect, the second is how you effectively problem-solve together.

Enquiry versus advocacy

The quality of problem-solving within your team can be quickly assessed by simply observing a meeting and noticing how much team members advocate for their own opinion, as opposed to listening, engaging and building on the ideas of their colleagues. Taking an enquiry, rather than advocacy approach, assists in collaborative problem solving and helps keep communication constructive and positive.

If you are finding it difficult to move people away from focusing on their opinions to fully exploring the presenting issue, try using a problem-solving tool. There is a plethora of these available. Force-field analysis, mind mapping, Ishikawa and cost-benefit analysis are just a small selection. These provide a structure that allows the issues to be worked through in a more objective and comprehensive way. Having someone within, or external to the team, to take on the facilitator role is also useful as they can stand back and focus on the process rather than the personalities.

Communicating with a solution in mind

To take on an enquiry approach we need to consider the language we use when communicating about problems.

Using solution-focused questioning is a useful way of concentrating on what is possible rather than what is not working. It also lessens arguments emerging about what members believe should or should not happen.

Solution-focused questions are open-ended 'how' or 'W' questions (what, when, where, who) that are framed towards the solution rather than the problem.

Some examples are:

- What would it look like if this was working for us?
- How do we want it to be different?
- How would it look if we achieved our goal?
- How can our strengths be used to resolve this?
- How do we build on what XYZ just suggested?
- What did we do last time that worked that could work again?
- What tells us that we can manage this?
- What is the first step we need to take towards resolution?
- How will we know we are progressing?
- Where can we get access to support for this?

Placing attention on what the team would like, rather than what is wrong, effectively generates energy more quickly towards potential solutions. Ideas generated can then be translated into next actions. In a way, it is starting with the endpoint in mind. Adoption of this type of communication by all members can quickly create impetus, both for immediate and longer-term problem resolution.

For solution-focused questioning to work people need to believe they have had some time to air their concerns. If not, they may think that there is no understanding of what the team is experiencing. Without empathy around the perceived reality it can be difficult to get people to change their focus towards option generation. Generally, this is not an issue for within-team communication as the problems are experienced together and so there is already a shared appreciation of them.

Creating space for joint problem solving

As workloads increase it seems that less time is being allocated to planning and joint problem solving. Operational activity takes over and people lament not having space to think strategically. In some situations, teams can feel in crisis management mode. They feel that they are dealing with recurring problems in the same manner as there is no time to step back and take a look at the bigger picture. In leadership training this is referred to as creating the space to 'get off the dance floor and stand on the balcony'.

Some practical ideas to introduce more effective team problem solving include:

- Allocating time within team meetings to discuss current key challenges and how these can be managed. Too often meetings are more of an information update or exchange. As time together can be limited, using it to advantage in problem solving is so much more valuable that sharing information that can be communicated in other ways
- Developing skills in problem solving and using mapping tools to facilitate this, as suggested above. Structured processes can help with efficiency and effectiveness, as long as there is a flexible approach to their use. Following the steps systematically when this is not needed can make it more about the process than the original problem

- Giving people information or questions to reflect on in advance. Ironically brainstorming, a popular approach to spontaneously coming up with and building on ideas, has been found to be more effective when people consider the issues before the session
- Scheduling some time to spend on planning regardless of how high the workload is and how many can attend. It can be a rare event for all of the team to be available.

These ideas are simple but not necessarily easy to implement when you are busy.

Quick Quip

"I am pulled so much into other people's crises and agendas I don't have time to think about what my team should really be doing." (Manager).

Exercise – Creating space to plan

Questions	Reflections
What gets in the way of shared planning and problem solving in your team and what can you do about it?	

Persisting despite set-backs

We often use the phrase 'bounce back' when we talk about resilience. Interestingly, the term itself is derived from the Latin word *re-salire*, which means 'jump'.

When we refer to resilience in this way, the implication is that it involves persisting and overcoming adversity.

To be persistent we need to have the energy to keep going despite obstacles.

We also need to move into action rather than stay in helplessness. Within teams this means that team members need to continue to provide, and draw on each other's, energy. A term often used to describe this determination is grit.

The energy levels of team members are likely to be variable with some more motivated and able to persist at particular times. Sometimes, energy may need to come from external support networks. As with many of the other components of the R@W Team, it is collective effort and responsibility that makes the difference. If the leader or only one or two members are taking the lead on energising and motivating others it may not be sustainable.

There also needs to be the capacity to reality check as to whether persistence is realistic. A stoical approach that involves persistence without considering the fall-out on relationships or health is counter-productive, as is persisting because of ego or reputation. Knowing what to persist with and how long to do so is the key. Deciding and reviewing this key aspect together as a group is essential.

Quick Quip

"Energy and persistence alter all things." (Benjamin Franklin).

Case study – ego and stoicism

The factory was no longer viable and workers knew this. Nevertheless, they decided that unless they were retrenched they would wait until the doors actually closed and walk out united. They had been a family and would stay that way until the end.

Persisting while denying reality and not exploring other opportunities is not resilience.

Exercise – Grit

Questions	Reflections
Where does the energy for persistence come from in your team?	

 Top Tips

Generate positivity

Positive energy is good for health, relationships and performance. Investing in 'feel good' and fun team activities makes good business sense.

Lighten up and have fun

Develop ways to lighten up when team members are taking themselves too seriously, or the impact of issues faced is being blown out of proportion. Create perspective. Recognise too that humour is a great stress de-fuser.

Engender optimism

Appreciate the reality of the challenges faced, but talk about them as temporary setbacks. More importantly, work together on a plan to address them. Keep the negative news compartmentalised and try not to let it overshadow the positive things that are happening.

Savour the good times

Let good news be contagious. Spend time discussing and reflecting on achievements, compliments and positive experiences. Positivity breeds positivity.

Damage control the dementers

Avoid getting pulled into the narrative of pessimists. Respectfully limit the airtime given to their negativity rather than attempt to change their opinions. The more issues your team is experiencing the more they can pull others into their view of the world.

Tackle problem solving by asking questions differently

Change the way your team talks about problems. Rather than getting stuck in the 'isn't it awful conversations' encourage questions that focus on what can be done about the issue. Try 'what is the first step we could take to fix this?' rather than 'what obstacles do you see with this?'

Learn the art of problem solving

Work on improving the processes you use to discuss problems and make decisions. Use decision-making tools, facilitate discussion and promote members enquiring and building on other people's ideas, rather than arguing for their own viewpoint. The quality of communication when there are conflicting views is a good indicator of team effectiveness overall. Value group decision-making and create space for this to occur.

Practise the serenity prayer

Minimise spending energy on concerns that you can't do anything about. Focus on what you can control and influence. This helps with managing uncertainty as well as focusing attention on what is important.

Know when to change tack

We are hard wired to try harder when events aren't going our way. We need to know when to do this and when we need to try something totally different or leave that issue and tackle another one. Persistence without acknowledging the negative consequences can breed arrogance or self-destruction.

Notes

| Chapter 8

 | **Self-care**

T4 Self-care

Promoting and deploying good stress management routines and being alert to overload in members.

Supporting life-work balance.

Part of developing a resilient team involves attention to how its members are supported in managing the pressure of work, whether this is caused by long hours, difficult customers or tasks with short deadlines or high complexity.

Establishing a culture of self-care

Workplace culture can be described as the character and personality of our organisations. It is the sum of our employees' values, traditions, beliefs, interactions, behaviors and attitudes. More often it is described as the unwritten rules by which we operate. Within teams we have sub-cultures that can be similar or quite different from other areas of our organisation.

When we talk about establishing a culture of self-care we are referring to the unwritten rules that determine how we care about the well-being of our colleagues.

In a practical sense this largely involves setting clear boundaries and expectations around workload and ensuring that work practices preserve, rather than inhibit, our health and well-being.

While the strategies for your team will be role specific, typical examples include:

- Regularly scheduling work breaks
- Ensuring holidays are taken
- Arranging meetings within core work hours, rather than too early or late
- Flexible working conditions to assist in accommodating personal lives
- Starting and leaving work at what could be considered a reasonable time
- Setting clear expectations of out-of-hours availability as well as work to be done at home
- Having time-out activities in the lunch room such as jigsaws or colouring in books –activities that engage a different part of the brain and promote stress relief
- Establishing on-site recreation or gyms
- Technology protocols, for example use of email and mobile phones
- Capacity for on-demand de-briefing following difficult incidents
- Explicit professional boundaries for work that involves direct care of others
- Regularly reviewing workload and role demands
- Rostering in a way that maximises recovery and ensures adequate sleep.

Open discussion and agreement within the team around management of pressures and work-home boundaries helps create an environment where self-care is seen as important.

Quick Quip

"Our work is emotionally gruelling and the pace is unrelenting. Taking some time out to do some colouring in refreshes me enough to manage the next task. We weren't sure of the idea initially but everyone has got into it so it's seen as acceptable." (Criminal lawyer).

Considering the physical and mental health of the team is also important. Possible actions include:

- Access to healthy eating alternatives in lunch rooms and at meetings and events
- Stand up desks
- Well-being and stress management programs
- Specific skill training – for example in mindfulness
- Employee assistance programs
- Organisational fitness initiatives
- Walk and talk meetings.

Ideally, organisations have policies and programs that support employees' well-being. To guarantee translation to the work unit level however, they should be role-modelled and supported by the team leader. This will ensure they become part of the 'way things are done around here'. Managers who tell their employees not to work on a weekend but then greet staff with a pile of emails from them first thing on Monday morning, are giving the message that you need to work on weekends to stay ahead of the game.

Case study – policy versus culture in self-care

A young professional, Georgina worked in a small office-based team. She enjoyed the role, and her colleagues, and was very passionate about what she was doing.

The workload was high and there was never enough time to complete all of the tasks. Georgina had children in child-care and needed to leave the office on time each day to pick them up. Her co-workers encouraged her to leave but stayed behind late themselves.

The organisation promoted taking a lunch break and not working on weekends but the reality within this team was quite different. One day, Georgina looked around at her colleagues and realised that they were all married to the job, frequently tired and with various medical conditions. She decided that the role was ideal for her but the culture was not. While people encouraged her to take lunch and leave on time she felt unable to do this without feeling guilty. The policy said one thing but the behaviours said something else. Georgina resigned.

Top Tips

In developing a culture of self-care it's not what you *say*, it's what you *do* that matters.

Emerging trends in de-briefing and recovery

As customers become more demanding, workplaces need to put more emphasis on supporting people to manage difficult encounters.

Support can range from impromptu debriefs with colleagues, who drop what they are doing to assist, to regular scheduled de-briefing or access to employee assistance programs.

Another emerging area, arising out of the hectic pace of work activity, is a need for recovery time. Sustaining high levels of performance over long periods without some type of break can be detrimental.

Quick Quip

"We used to be able to take a breather between the events we run. Now we are straight into the next one and are on the run all of the time. We warn people when we recruit them that once they can't sustain the pace any longer they'll have to leave."

There are a variety of ways in which recovery can be built into team routines. Taking holidays or flexi-days is an obvious one, as is planning work so that unusually intense activity, for example in event staging or end of year finances, is followed by a day or two where work is less intense. Recovery can also be built into the day with regular breaks and mini-relaxations or reflection time.

Case study – pamper day

Marianne ran a team that worked with difficult clients experiencing stressful circumstances. Most of the work was out of the office with staff members mainly working independently. The team was hard working and enthusiastic about their work, sometimes overstepping the boundaries of their role in order to help their clients.

Marianne had high expectations of performance but was also known as supportive. She kept a check on how the team was faring and occasionally, when she could see people were struggling, she would call what became known as a 'pamper day'. While most of us would imagine this to be one of indulgence, a pamper day for this team was a client free day doing administrative tasks and sharing lunch. This routine of time out became both a conduit for recovery and team bonding.

Top Tips

Recovery time is crucial in some roles to prevent burnout.

Being alert to early warning signs

A useful aspect in promoting self-care is awareness of early symptoms of overload. This involves knowing co-workers well enough to be able to determine when they are not themselves and appearing, for example, more withdrawn or easily agitated. Noticing and offering support in these circumstances is valuable. Many team members also give each other a 'heads up' when they have personal issues that may impact on their behaviour or performance so that others can better understand what is happening and not take the changes in demeanour personally.

Case study – survivor

A team decided to have their own version of the TV series 'Survivor' and manufactured an elaborate jungle torch. Whenever anyone's stress was starting to impact on others the torch would appear in his or her office. This was the signal for them to take a day off. They had been voted off the island!

It is also useful for members to share what works best when they are overwhelmed so that this action can be supported – for example taking a five-minute break outside or switching tasks completely. Some people even love to clean the kitchen as it is something they have complete control over!

Quick Quip

"When I have had a really stressful time at work I go home and dig a hole. I get a work out, achieve something and have total control over what I am doing."

Case study – preparing for a busy period

A research and development team was about to go through four months of unusually high workload. Already working hard, they were anxious at how they might survive this. They spent a morning planning strategies on how to best deal with the stressful time ahead.

As part of the planning, they shared their early signs of overload and gave each other permission to express concern and offer support when these were evident.

The team also shared which strategies were most useful for them to de-stress during work hours and gave each other permission to engage in these. Some needed time out for a walk; others mini-meditation time; some a conversation; and some just the ability to switch to a less onerous task.

The group also discussed boundaries around work hours, what they needed from their managers and the agreed processes for regular regrouping on project progress and priorities. They also developed their personal outside-of-work relaxation outlets and stress management plans.

Top Tips

Planning workload management together supports well-being and creates joint responsibility for stress management.

Managing mental health issues

An additional challenge when considering the well-being of staff is how to best manage mental health issues. With one in five of us expected to experience mental illness in our lifetime, it is an increasingly common occurrence to be working with colleagues who are managing such a condition. While specific discussions on accommodating this generally needs to be kept confidential it is important to consider the impact of changed working arrangements on the rest of the team. It is also prudent to have an agreed timeframe for review of any duty modifications and to share what can be shared with the team. Open-ended arrangements that place additional pressure on others can cause perceived inequity or ultimately resentment. This can run counter to recovery and longer-term management. If you are a manager, seeking professional advice on how to assist your staff member may be helpful.

Negotiating roles

One consequence of having declining staff or resources is that roles, rather than just workloads, may need revisiting. Teams are increasingly reflecting on what it is they *have* to do versus what it is that they would *like* to do. Groups who have blurred work boundaries, who have customer expectations beyond what is possible, or who take on all the tasks that do not fit elsewhere within an organisation, may find this more of an issue.

Case study – negotiating role boundaries

A professional team providing government services found itself in a position where many activities that did not fit easily into the roles of the other divisions in the department were allocated to them. The issue was made worse by the appointment of a new manager with an accommodating style. She took on new work eagerly – keen to show her competence and the capacity of her team. Over time this resulted in considerable pressure on her staff and a reputation of being incompetent as it simply wasn't possible to deliver on all of the tasks allocated.

Top Tips

Maintaining boundaries around roles becomes more important when job demands continue to build without a corresponding increase in resources.

Exercise – Self-care in practice

Questions	Reflections
What team practices and routines assist in stress management?	
What shared expectations exist around work hours, workloads, out of hour activity and breaks?	

Questions	Reflections
How can members better look out for each other and 'temperature check' on how people are faring?	
Is recovery time needed and if so how is it built in?	

Promoting life-work balance

The capacity for life-work balance is generally seen as an important aspect of self-care. This has become almost illusive for those experiencing long hours and constant connectivity through technology advances. The advent of mobile devices has fundamentally changed the nature of what constitutes a typical working day. The upside is the flexibility that remote working enables, while the flip side is constant accessibility. Difficulties in separating work and home life has led to the concept often being labelled work-life integration, in recognition that both aspects need to coexist.

Negotiating boundaries around response times and accessibility is useful but can be difficult if there is not team agreement on this. If a manager promotes no contact over the weekend yet sends emails and texts the messages become mixed.

An over-emphasis on time spent at work, accessibility and flexibility around hours often deflects from the true meaning of balance – the capacity to do the things that matter most to us.

Many people work long hours yet thrive on this, as it is a very important part of their life. Others find even a few additional hours a week detract from activities they would rather be doing, or people they want to spend time with.

What constitutes a balanced life will vary across the life span as priorities and interests shift. We will be more likely to feel there is less life-work conflict when work does not get in the way of what is important to us. It could be a hobby, time with friends or family, attending school activities or assisting in the care of elderly parents.

In taking this approach to life-work balance the strategy is for team members to identify what is important to them and to put boundaries in place to stop work getting in the way of this. Ideally, intentions are shared and supported by the team. Examples might be recognising events and activities important to colleagues and assisting them to ensure work does not intrude on these. To work effectively this needs perceived equity for all, as well as boundaries that still ensure jobs are completed.

Accommodating the personal lives of others is also a part of the 'connected' component of the R@W Team and is explored more in Chapter 10.

Balancing self-care with performance

Attention to personal self-care has to be balanced by flexibility and a willingness to put in effort and provide additional back up support when it is needed. It's a case of ensuring mutual support *plus* mutual accountability in a team. Open-ended support that is not reciprocated or managed by the team can eventually cause resentment if it places more pressure on others.

In cases where an organisation has become less generous in its flexibility and care for staff this can sometimes be more difficult for staff than if they had not had these conditions in the first place. As budgets tighten and expectations change some employees are experiencing this happening.

Quick Quip

"This university is no longer a benevolent employer." (Senior academic).

Case study – one-way flexibility

Belinda managed a group of professionals who had transferred from demanding positions in search of less stress and greater flexibility in working hours. Their new organisation had generous and varied leave options, as well as the capacity to work remotely and have flexible working hours. Over time, the team started to take advantage by taking leave more often, as well as leaving regularly for family and personal appointments. Belinda struggled as she felt the team were under-performing. They, in turn, believed that they were perfectly entitled to the leave and actively supported each other in what they saw as a healthy approach to life-work balance.

 Top Tips

Develop stress busters

Design joint, as well as individual strategies, to manage the everyday stress of the job. Promote these as expected, rather than desirable, expectations of the team and of its manager.

Embed specific techniques for gruelling jobs

If your team's role has specific challenges such as angry customers, physical threat or high emotional labour, ensure bespoke supports are in place. Regular de-briefing and training in techniques to minimise personal physical and psychological harm are essential.

Recognise the value of recovery

Think like an athlete and know when time out is needed for rejuvenation. Agree on boundaries around the working day, after-hours access, breaks and holidays. Organise schedules so that intense periods are offset with tasks of less intensity. Make sure these enhance performance and do not become entitlements that people expect and become inflexible about.

Be alert to tipping points

Share how you act when you are overloaded and give your colleagues permission to alert you when these behaviours are evident. Offer a hand and support each other when these symptoms are observed.

Regularly check-in on workload

Put in place team processes that allow regular review of workloads and other challenges being faced. Re-visit expectations and how tasks are being allocated and shared.

Have a life

Know what constitutes life-work balance for yourself and your co-workers. Support work not getting in the way of what is important to each other outside of the job. Share what is symbolic of work taking over, for example not getting to engage in a particular hobby, or spending time with particular people.

Notes

| Chapter 9
 | **Capability**

T5 Capability

Continually building capacity through accessing networks and supports.

Seeking feedback and building on what works well.

A team cannot be effective if it does not have the capability to do the tasks assigned to it. Much of the elements that create capability such as skills and team processes have been covered in other chapters - in particular those exploring the 'robust', 'resourceful' and 'alignment' aspects of the R@W Team. In this section we focus on the increased need for teams to regularly review their capability against the changes occurring around them. The more volatile the team's operating environment, the more important this factor becomes.

Reviewing capability involves regularly seeking feedback about team performance and adjusting activity to align with this. Sometimes this may require a change in skill or knowledge. When there is limited capacity to recruit new talent then teams need to extend their existing capability by accessing support outside of the group itself. Extending team capabilities though linkages to external networks is a smart way of building resources without needing to buy or hire them.

Seeking and acting on feedback

The starting point for seeking feedback is to identify and prioritise the team's stakeholders. Customers are the obvious ones but teams generally have other groups, managers or bodies that they serve. These may be within or outside of the organisation.

If formal feedback mechanisms such as sales, employee or customer surveys or service agreement key performance indicators are not in place, it may be useful to discuss how meaningful feedback can be regularly and easily collected. Without some sort of assessment of how well your team is operating against changing environmental conditions, it can risk becoming out of touch, or even redundant.

Teams may also need access to quantitative data to assess performance within their market or sector. Benchmarking, market share, and other statistical information are just some examples. The challenge is to determine how to source data that is accurate and relevant, and then to determine how it can inform performance at a team level.

Top Tips

You can't stay relevant and add value unless you know what your customers want.

Case study – lack of direction and feedback

A policy team worked in a centralised function, fairly removed from its customers and community and within a large organisation. The scope of potential work was complex and vast and there were competing stakeholder needs. The team had many long-term projects that would be placed on and off hold at management request, and rarely received feedback on the direct impact of its output. As a result, members were uncertain of where priorities should be, and if their work was adding any actual value. They also felt that their work was neither understood nor appreciated.

The team decided to take more control over prioritising by routinely meeting with stakeholders to define how they could best add value within allocated funding and changing external demands. As a result, they were better able to prioritise tasks and assess the impact of what they were doing.

To seek feedback is one imperative, to act on it is another. If you are asking for the opinions of others, you need to ensure that you are able to respond in some way. When there is no capacity to resolve criticism directed at the team, the challenge becomes how best to collectively manage it. It is still better to know what you are dealing with rather than avoid hearing bad news.

Quick Quip

"Why would I seek feedback when we get plenty of negative comments directed at us all of the time? You have to become immune to complaints in this job."

Exercise – Asking and responding to feedback

Questions	Reflections
How does your team know how well it is performing? What feedback does it seek and from whom?	

Questions	Reflections
How does your team act on feedback it receives?	

Building capability through networks

In times where recruitment of additional staff is not possible despite increasing demands, teams need ways to build capability within existing funding. One way to do this is to link into networks and relationships outside of the team either within, or external, to the organisation. This can extend the knowledge and skill of the team with minimal financial cost.

These relationships can have a variety of purposes. Examples include access to technical or professional advice, industry trends and also more ready access to related services. Ideally the approach should be strategic, identifying who the team needs relationships with to better perform its job. Members can then share the responsibility for establishing and maintaining these contacts.

It is important to note that it is the quality not the quantity of people within the network that is important. Also, ensure that you offer some sort of reciprocation for the advice or access provided and that relationships are actively maintained.

Case study – external networks

A social services team working with clients with complex needs was highly dependent on being able to refer clients onto other services. Referral was much quicker when a person from that organisation was known and could be contacted directly, rather than going through call centres.

For many years a coordinator had been assigned responsibility for ensuring referral networks were current but the role was abolished following a restructure. Over a period of months, the relationships needed with other organisations declined. This greatly compromised the work of the team. They realised that they needed to restore these relationships to perform the work effectively. As workloads were high they divided responsibility for this in order to make it viable.

Top Tips

Teams need to be linked into external supports in the same way that individuals need a personal support network.

Case study – smart leveraging

The health promotion team had an ambitious and well-funded project that involved training teams across a number of organisations on how to implement workplace well-being initiatives in-house. Over-night the budget was slashed and it seemed that the project was no longer viable. There were funds to support only a handful of organisations, meaning that there would not be enough traction to produce any meaningful impact.

The team had the idea of supporting industry bodies to implement the initiatives. This was a smart solution that allowed greater coverage of the working population. A few strategic partnerships allowed the project goals to still be achieved.

Developing member access to support and advice

As discussed above, one way of increasing the team's capability is to link into external support networks. This principle also extends to individuals. It could take the form of mentoring, debriefing, technical advice and any other type of assistance that helps members perform effectively. If you are a manager it is very difficult to be the sole provider of support to your staff. Linking them into the maximum assistance you can find makes your job easier.

Case study – linking team members into support

Sarah was an experienced and well-respected manager. While highly competent, she realised the importance of having a strong personal support network. Over time, she built up a group of people who served this purpose.

As she was highly empathetic and approachable, Sarah's staff saw her as a major source of support for them and she found that she was spending considerable time providing this. With a demanding role herself, she began to realise that she was limited in the assistance she could feasibly provide. Instead, she focused on assisting her team members to establish their own support networks. These included a group of external mentors, coaches, counsellors and trainers, many of whom were not paid but were offered some type of reciprocation from the team.

Exercise – Linking into external resources

Questions	Reflections
What external networks or relationships are important to team performance?	
How are necessary relationships built and maintained?	

◯ Top Tips

Ask how the team is performing

With operating environments changing rapidly it more important than ever to check in on how the team is meeting the needs of those it serves. Put in place processes that allow you to get feedback from your key stakeholders – both within and outside of your organisation. Determine who you need feedback from and why, and who is responsible for getting this.

Act on the intelligence you gather

Develop a way for the team to share the feedback it has received and then act on it. Asking people's opinions without responding creates expectations that need to be managed.

Take responsibility for your personal supports

It is difficult to manage a challenging role without a network of supports, both at work and at home. If you are a manager do not try to provide all of the assistance yourself. Link your staff into what they need where you can and encourage each person to develop networks for themselves.

Develop and use your networks strategically

Teams can build their capabilities substantially through linking into outside networks. Discuss what knowledge, skill and support the team requires and work on developing relationships with other individuals or organisations.

| Notes

| Chapter 10

 | **Connected**

T6 Connected

Caring for colleagues as people and being co-operative and supportive with each other.

Resilient teams feel a sense of connection with each other. They work on developing an environment where members are actively supported and feel cared about as people. While each person knows they are accountable for their contribution there is appreciation and understanding that everyone has a life out of work that deserves consideration.

Creating a sense of belonging

There is little doubt that a feeling of belonging builds resilience. We only need to look at post-disaster efforts to notice how important a sense of community is for recovery. Whenever there are floods, droughts, fires or other major events people rally around to help each other and it is the community spirit that helps people through the tragedy.

While we are not generally dealing with life-threatening events in our jobs the sense of belonging is still important. At work this is mostly created within the group in which we work, rather than the organisation as a whole. If we feel welcomed and part of the team this builds our capacity to manage challenges as we have confidence that 'we are all in this together'.

We establish connection through the everyday interactions we have with our colleagues. Simple actions such as greeting each other warmly and taking time to share some aspect of what is happening in our lives all assists in developing positive relationships and camaraderie.

If members feel like outsiders, or even isolated, this can impact on their resilience and may even prompt them to leave. It also fractures the group, especially if sub-groups have developed.

The strong interpersonal relationships we have with colleagues can become a major part of our job satisfaction and commitment. Sometimes our sense of belonging can shift after staffing changes, especially when the newly formed team has different views on what to do and how to go about it (the 'robust' component). It is not unusual when a number of people leave a small cohesive team for others to follow.

Promoting organisational belonging

There are numerous ways to create a workforce that identifies closely with being part of an organisation. These can range from corporate clothing and social functions to service awards and community social responsibility programs. The focus in this book however is on aspects that are within the team's direct influence.

The double-edged sword of belonging occurs when an organisation has a very strong community and has to close down for financial or market reasons. In these cases, people sometimes refer to co-workers as part of the family. In such circumstances the challenge becomes finding ways to continue the existing relationships, or ensure that new ones are formed to replace them. This is also a common challenge for people who retire after long-standing employment with one company.

Exercise – Creating a sense of belonging

Questions	Reflections
What can the team do to increase a sense of belonging?	

Establishing mutual support and cooperation

An important element of resilience within teams is the existence of mutual support. In effective teams they understand the importance of giving each other assistance without needing to be asked. It engenders collective responsibility for outcomes as well as a strong sense of cohesion.

What comprises support will vary across job functions and teams but what is important is that people readily offer assistance to each other but are also happy to ask for, and accept, help.

Case study – preserving a supportive culture

A team was going through a very challenging period. Over a period of a year or so they experienced an increase in the number of clients at the same time as losing several experienced team members.

Whilst the expansion in client numbers was seen as positive, members were finding it stressful to continue to maintain professional standards while up-skilling new workers and dealing with backlogs in the administrative work. People were tired and concerned at how long they could continue to spread themselves so thinly. All persisted largely because of their strong belief in the job they were doing.

At a planning day the team acknowledged that a major part of their coping mechanism was their caring for each other and that this in turn enabled them to provide high quality care to their clients. Planned growth in employee numbers was seen as potentially having a detrimental impact on the strong sense of belonging within the team. They subsequently discussed the actions that made them a caring team and agreed to maintain these as well as to add some others. Care was an aspect of their culture that they saw as crucial and important to maintain.

Providing support without being asked

In teams where mutual support is embedded, people provide support willingly and without being asked.

The type of support needed within a team will be unique but typical examples include:

- Providing a safe place to debrief difficult events or encounters, for example angry customers
- Practical back-up in getting tasks done on time or out of hours
- Sharing of job-related knowledge or skill
- Emotional support during periods of high stress
- Idea or perspective sharing
- Advice on how to navigate the organisational politics or processes
- Providing access to networks outside of the team
- Advocacy around issues
- Flexibility in availability.

The importance of reciprocation

One-way support does not generally work as when individuals are providing regular help without reciprocation they can eventually become annoyed or resentful. This is especially the case where workload and stress levels are already high. Often people will stop helping after a while and retreat into focusing on their own responsibilities.

The rewards of generosity

Going out of our way to provide back-up or other types of assistance is also a tangible demonstration of consideration and respect towards our colleagues. Often when team relationships become fractured, common courtesies and simple acts of support are the first to disappear.

Psychology researchers also tell us that generosity is good for us and improves our personal health and well-being. After we perform an act of altruism we experience a rush of euphoria followed by a longer period of calmness. This triggering of endorphins is termed 'helper's high'.

Accepting support graciously

Mutual support not only implies that we need to pay back favours, it also means that we need to be willing to accept help when it is given. Frequently refusing the support given by our colleagues can be seen negatively. Our refusal is, in essence, the giving back of a gift. It is not only ungracious but can create an impression that we are above needing help from others.

'Why don't you ever let anyone help you'? (Exasperated response to another refusal of assistance).

Asking for support readily

Many of us are happy to assist others but less inclined to ask for help when we could use it ourselves. Independence, ego or simply fear of being judged or looking incompetent can get in the way. Being stoical and continuing to soldier on alone works against resilience. What we need to appreciate is that asking for help when we need it is a strength and not a weakness.

Within teams it is important to develop an environment where it is okay to be vulnerable. We can develop this by setting up an expectation that questions are asked and assistance is requested. The unwritten message needs to be that no matter how competent or talented we are, we all need to check in on whether we are on track and ask for support at some stage. Setting up such a work environment requires role modelling by the team's leader. If leaders encourage team members to do this without doing it personally, it sends a mixed message around competence.

Workplaces that are highly competitive, where we need to look competent all the time and where we feel judged if we need assistance, all work counter to asking for support. Some occupations have a poorer track record than others in this respect. Such environments may not only increase employee stress, but also impact on personal confidence and even mental health.

A concept that is becoming popular in leadership development circles is 'confident vulnerability'. This involves team members recognising and working with their strengths but also being able to be vulnerable when they need to be and ask for help.

Case study – the need for vulnerability

Serena unexpectedly became the carer for her grandchild at about the same time as she took on a new, and challenging, managerial role. Many of her colleagues and friends were quick to offer help but Serena declined. Her rationale was that she should be able to manage the situation herself and she did not want to stretch friendships through imposing on others.

Some months later she realised that she needed to admit her vulnerability and ask for help. She arranged a catch-up with each of those who had offered support to discuss what would be reasonable for them. Of course they all offered assistance, after all they had done that already. Serena just needed to ask for it.

Within teams, allowing people to be vulnerable around their personal as well as their work life promotes a shared understanding that members all have a life outside of work that needs to be appreciated.

Case study – the stress of invulnerability

The grand round of a public hospital became known as the 'walk of fear' by trainee doctors. Giving any indication that you were unsure, or didn't understand, was perceived as risky as it suggested to others that you were not competent. Questions that should have been asked were withheld and there was a heavy psychological toll on members of the medical team. It was stressful working in an environment where concerns could not be voiced and professional advice and support was not forthcoming. It was also a patient safety issue.

Exercise – Establishing mutual support

Questions	Reflections
What does mutual support look like in your team?	
What gets in the way of asking for or giving support?	

Top Tips

Mutual back-up and support between team members is important in collectively managing challenging work.

Accommodating Personal Lives

While we need to be supportive of each other in getting the job done, we also need to be considerate of out-of-work lives.

In the chapter on self-care, we discussed the need to support team members in having a reasonable level of life-work balance. This involved being appreciative of what is important in their lives and supporting them to make sure that work does not intrude excessively on this.

Equally, we need to be accommodating of circumstances that impact on people's performance such as changes in health, living arrangements, relationships, financial and family issues. As discussed in Chapter 6, this can only be achieved when support is also balanced by accountability. This generally means that any flexibility or changes in work requirements should be time-limited, with a review.

The opposite of an environment where there is care for our personal lives occurs in teams where people feel that *who* they are is less relevant than *what* they are there to do. Not only is there lack of interest in people's identities and lives there can also be no attempt to develop any sense of camaraderie within the team.

Quick Quip

"I feel like a function not a person."

The actions of managers set the tone for how successfully personal lives are accommodated in teams.

Quick Quip

"You are the first manager I have had who has acknowledged that I have a life outside of work."

The impact of interpersonal conflict

One of the main obstacles to creating co-operation within a team is interpersonal conflict and a lack of trust or respect. These aspects are explored in the next chapter.

⚙ Top Tips

Help people feel they belong

Being welcoming and inclusive is an essential part of teamwork. It also builds resilience as people feel that they are part of a community that is working together, in contrast to trying to manage independently.

Identify what mutual support looks like in your team

In each team, the types of support that are needed will differ. Identify what support your members need to provide and agree on expectations around this.

Build a culture of care

When we get stressed we become more inwardly focused and less considerate of others. Our own needs tend to dominate. Develop a working environment where people look out for each other and are accepting of differences. Tolerance is a value that is becoming less common in workplaces these days.

Enable confident vulnerability

We want our team members to be confident in their strengths but we also want them to feel that they can ask for help when they need it. Establish this within your team by allowing people to question and admit inadequacies without being judged as incompetent. Take up the philosophy that 'there's no such thing as a stupid question'.

Accommodate personal lives

Most of us will have events occur in our home lives that spill over onto our performance at work. When colleagues help us out through these times, by taking on more or covering our rosters, it helps us feel valued. It develops an environment where we feel we are a person not a number.

| Chapter 11

 | **Alignment**

T7 Alignment

Aligning and developing the talents of team members to create the desired outcomes.

Sharing and celebrating success with each other.

Achieving the R@W component of 'alignment' involves team members creating a shared version of success and motivating each other towards it by noticing and acknowledging progress. It also involves maximising skill and knowledge sharing and promptly resolving interpersonal conflicts that could create misalignment.

Seeking out and acknowledging progress

Noticing progress

As work goals become more ambitious, or simply less achievable following workplace budget cuts or changes, a critical factor in sustaining motivation is ensuring that team members feel they are making some progress.

We seem to be hardwired at work to focus more on what hasn't been done rather than what has been completed. We let the deficits outweigh the strengths.

When you had your last performance review did you spend time congratulating yourself on what was rated well, or did you focus straight away on the development goals? When you review your daily task list do you worry about what is outstanding, or feel good about what you have actioned? When we are busy we can sometimes find that any sense of progress is overshadowed by what is yet to be done.

Feeling that you are going backwards, or simply not progressing, is personally de-motivating. When this feeling is at a team level it can lead to poor morale and a belief that desired outcomes are unachievable.

A simple activity to highlight success is a variation of the well-known 'count your blessings' exercise where you write down daily what you are thankful for. It's a way of introducing gratitude into your life and appreciating what you have. It involves teams asking themselves 'What went well today and why'? The 'why' component of this question is important as it emphasises what the team actually did to gain the positive outcome. The idea is that by highlighting this behaviour you can appreciate and build on it.

Top Tips

Sometimes not going backwards is progress when you have also had to deal with unexpected events.

Case study – file overload

Within the office of the ombudsman staff were overloaded. There were far more complaints than there were people to respond to them. Each complaint had a hard copy file and these were piled up on the desks. After a meeting one day the staff decided to store all of the files in the cupboard and bring them out one at a time as they actioned them. The work was still backed-up but the constant visual reminder was gone, bringing less anxiety and a better sense of control over the workload.

Defining progress

In order to recognise progress, we firstly need to define it. In some jobs this is obvious as there is an end or completion point. Builders, for example, have a tangible outcome to show for their effort. On the other hand, someone taking a complaint on the phone is simply rewarded with another complaint once they have resolved the first.

"At least when I am on the tractor at home I can achieve something when I go around in circles."

Perhaps you have a job where positive outcomes are infrequent, or the contribution you are able to make lacks significance in the bigger scheme of things. Some jobs in social services and not-for-profit agencies can be characterised in this way, as the public need is often greater than the capacity to help.

In the cases where progress is less obvious it is important to define or reframe what success is so that it can then be acknowledged.

Quick Quip

"Our manager set up a spread sheet to track our progress on projects as we are so far behind. The workload is so unrealistic we call it our failure sheet."

Case study – reframing adding value

A large team of nurses were employed to support new mothers in the weeks after their babies were delivered. Most were drawn to the job because of a passion for working with babies. Generally, the arrival of a new baby is a joyous affair and nurses have the opportunity to share in this. This team however worked in a disadvantaged area where many of the mothers were facing poverty, domestic violence, alcohol and drug abuse or depression. Often, after home visits, the nurses felt quite distressed and questioned their capacity to make any difference to the lives of women who were facing such overwhelming obstacles. What became important was the need to reframe what adding value was. Rather than seeing that the problems were too overwhelming they started to focus on achieving small steps that were possible. While this did not solve all the problems of their clients it gave the nurses a sense that they had achieved something useful. They also felt more motivated in their job.

Top Tips

When what is needed is far beyond what you can do, sometimes you have to redefine success to stay motivated.

Acknowledging individual effort

Within a team there is scope to acknowledge effort for individuals and the team overall. Resilient teams do this in a way that creates alignment rather than competition.

We are all willing to do more and persist longer if we know that our input has been noticed and valued. We also feel a greater sense of contribution if milestones and successes are celebrated in some way. This is particularly the case in work that is the same each day, or where the outcomes are achieved over long timeframes.

Organisations often implement reward and recognition programs as part of a broader staff attraction and retention strategy. These are very valuable. However, this section focuses on recognition activities within the scope of most teams to implement.

It is out of scope for many teams to fund material rewards to acknowledge team member efforts, but there are many ways in which this can be done without a budget.

One of the most powerful ways of acknowledging colleagues is through genuine feedback that is specific and given in a timely manner.

Employees commonly expect recognition to come from their manager. While this is important, feedback from colleagues and customers is also very powerful.

A complement on our actions from a colleague we respect can mean the difference between a having a stressful or worthwhile day. Positive comments cost nothing and are extremely validating.

Frequent positive feedback in teams helps build a sense of feeling valued. This becomes even more important when positive feedback is largely absent from other sources, for example when interactions are mainly complaints or unpleasant encounters. Working in an outgoing call centre and ringing for donations is a good example of a role where customer responses can be disheartening.

Publicly providing feedback can heighten its impact. Formal acknowledgement at meetings or in emails, memos or newsletters are common examples. Others include allocation to interesting projects, flexibility in hours and access to training. It is useful for the team to discuss and provide ideas on how acknowledgement can be done in an equitable and motivating manner.

Quick Quip

"If we are going to work this hard, the least management could do is acknowledge it rather than just expect it."

Celebrating achievements and sharing successes

The celebration of achievements is important within teams as it provides acknowledgement that people have reached significant goals together.

As discussed above, before you can celebrate achievements you may need to determine what constitutes an achievement for the team. When work has tangible outcomes or stages determining success is easy. When the work has no clear end point, or where successful outcomes are over a longer term or rare, identification of a point to celebrate can be difficult.

Recognising success assists a team in persevering as it demonstrates progress has been made. Celebrations also have the additional benefit of improving cohesion through providing an opportunity for social interaction, time out and highlighting purpose. Of course, the method of celebration will depend on the progress being acknowledged and the options open to the team.

Quick Quip

"It's easy to feel like we are failing as successful outcomes are rare in our job." (Child protection worker).

Case study – recognising achievements

It was coming up to Christmas and the Human Resources Director was reviewing the unit's annual progress in preparation for the end-of-year staff lunch. She listed a number of achievements that she knew her team had made but felt quite despondent as the list looked small when compared to the tasks on next year's agenda. Nevertheless, she emailed the list thanking her staff for their contribution.

When each staff member saw what was listed they added work that was not recorded. Before long there was a large number of achievements to celebrate. With the focus on the challenges that lay in front of them, they had lost sight of the progress they had already made.

Top Tips

It is easier to notice what we haven't done than recognise how far we have come.

Exercise – Acknowledging effort and success

Questions	Reflections
How does your team identify and acknowledge team member effort?	
What constitutes achievements in your team and how and when can these be celebrated?	

A factor that can work against alignment within a team is interpersonal conflict.

Resolving interpersonal conflicts early

Interpersonal conflict is often more common in demanding work environments. This is to be expected as when we are under stress our tolerance levels are lowered and our behaviour can deteriorate. Our worse traits can intensify and even our strengths can work against us. If we are very organised, for example, we can start to impose our needs more on colleagues. This can be seen as trying to control and exert authority over other people's work routines. If we are accommodating we may find ourselves giving in to others even more, thus creating more stress on ourselves.

Fundamental to managing conflict within groups, is a climate of open communication where we are able to say the things that need to be said about each other in a constructive way, and where feedback is listened to and acted upon. This requires a safe environment where team members can disagree without being fearful of being judged, or suffering retribution or other negative consequences. To achieve this, members need to be skilled in giving and receiving feedback.

A frequent obstacle in teams occurs when discontent is not voiced and goes underground. It reappears instead in behaviours that undermine effectiveness such as pursuing personal agendas that work against the common good of the group. Colleagues who are vocal in their discontent about work can more easily draw others into their views when there is tension within the team that is not being addressed.

Another factor to consider in conflict management on a team is a clearly defined escalation process for issues. This should commence with each member taking responsibility for having difficult conversations themselves, in the first instance, and not deferring this responsibility to the team's leader. Ideally, team members are given the skills to do this.

If a direct conversation does not work, a number of stages can be identified which may end up in external formal mediation. The further an interpersonal conflict escalates from its source, the more difficult it can be to resolve.

Case study – when small issues escalate

A group of around 20 women had worked together for a long time. Over the years, they had shared a lot about their personal lives with each other.

Clients reported high levels of customer service from the team and its members were well regarded. However, within the work area there was frequent conflict over small things. Often this became quite emotional as it involved friends falling out, sides being taken and divisions then forming within the team. Rumours were rampant and the boundaries between exchanging personal snippets and talking about people behind their backs became blurred.

Over time, the team had developed the belief that issues needed to be put in writing to be addressed. The team also viewed it as the manager's role to resolve any interpersonal conflict. As a result, small issues quickly escalated, leaving the manager trying to mediate around incidents that he had not directly observed. Frustrated with his perceived incompetence in these matters, staff often bypassed him and went directly to the director who had worked with most of the women a long time and was easily accessible in the workplace corridors.

With the help of an external facilitator, the group were given skills on positively closing down gossip and discussing issues with each other. A trial period was instigated of no written complaints and each member was given confidential feedback on aspects of their behaviour that they needed to maintain or change. A complaints escalation process was also developed.

The conflicts still occurred but they were less frequent and the energy spent on them was greatly diminished.

Top Tips

Conflict between team members needs to be addressed at its source, which means developing a climate where people feel safe to speak honestly and constructively say what needs to be said.

Exercise – Strategies for conflict resolution

Questions	Reflections
How do you make it safe to give personal criticism within your team?	

Questions	Reflections
How can you improve skills in resolving interpersonal conflict?	
What processes do you have for managing conflict on the team?	

Developing team member skill and knowledge

In the chapters on the components 'robust' and 'capability' we spoke of the need to recruit talent and build the capacity of the team through linkages to external resources. Within the component 'resourceful' we also explored the importance of harnessing the personal strengths of members.

Within an aligned team, members also willingly share their knowledge and skill and look to ways to cross-skill, and mentor or train each other.

Typical activities to develop talent using internal resources are:

- Job shadowing, where colleagues follow and observe each other
- Project debriefs and reviews where the learning around recent team activity is shared
- Mentoring (for example a 'buddy' arrangement on commencement in a role)
- Job rotation.

In fast-paced operating environments it is also important to anticipate new skills or knowledge that may be needed to stay viable. This is where access to external networks, as explored in Chapter 9, becomes important.

Exercise – Sharing team member experience

Questions	Reflections
What strategies are in place within your team to share knowledge and skill?	

By now you may be feeling exhausted just thinking about all of the elements that you could invest in within your team. As discussed at the beginning of this book, it is important to approach your plan in a strategic way. Identify the strengths that you can build on and consider what changes you can make that will have the most impact. In the next chapter you will be guided in how to do this.

 ## Top Tips

Notice progress

When the 'to do' list keeps growing it can be hard to believe you are making any inroads into the work. In this environment teams need to be more mindful of what progress looks like and how it can be acknowledged. When you feel like you are not moving forward it can be demoralising.

Recognise effort

An important way of valuing people is to personally recognise effort. A genuine and timely compliment from a colleague is worth gold and costs nothing. Explore ways in which you can recognise the contribution of members of your team, both formally and informally.

Celebrate the wins together

Celebrating achievements is an excellent way of acknowledging shared effort. If your projects are longer-term, these may need to be chunked down into significant milestones. This element is especially important if goals are ambitious and a lot of hard work is needed to reach them.

Share knowledge and experience

Look for ways to mentor and train each other. Be generous in sharing what you know. Avoid using knowledge as power.

Resolve conflicts early

Develop a team climate where it is safe for people to disagree and be honest with each other. Train members in how to give and receive criticism in a way that is constructive and builds strong relationships. Conflict not addressed can destroy teamwork. Discuss the team's expectations around open communication. Resolve conflict as it occurs and minimise reliance on formal processes. Once an issue escalates it becomes much harder to resolve.

Notes

Chapter 12

Putting together your team plan

Now that you have worked through the chapters and reflected on all aspects of the R@W Team components it is time to integrate your ideas into an overall plan.

Remember to include how you intend to maintain or build on what you are already doing well. Refresh your memory of current strategies by looking back at what you listed in Chapter 4.

As an example, you may have noted that one of the important actions you undertake are quarterly project de-brief meetings. If these assist with resilience they may form part of the maintenance aspect of the plan, especially if you have started to cancel them due to busyness. You may also build on the success of these by fine-tuning how they are conducted, or scheduling them more often.

The reflections and activities you have undertaken within each chapter should provide a range of ideas for your plan.

You can use the template below to outline your agreed actions within the team. Two sample plans are provided for additional direction should you need it.

Steps in developing your plan to build your resilience

Identify strategies that you already use effectively and list these in the table below. Then add new actions you have considered following reading this book. It is important to work together on this so that the plan is shared and owned. Be sure to make the actions tangible so that you will know if you have implemented them. Note too that some actions may need to be undertaken by the leader not the team. Sample plan 2 includes examples that fit in this category.

R@W Team Component	Action plan
Robust	
Resourceful	
Perseverance	
Self-care	
Capability	
Connected	
Alignment	

Sample plan 1

This example is of a situation where a senior leadership team is performing well, with reasonable levels of resilience. It has considerable challenges ahead however, due to major industry reforms.

R@W Team Component	Action plan
Robust	Conduct a planning day to define the new direction given funding changes. Ensure that our core purpose is not lost in this. Get more involved in lobbying around changes in the sector.
Resourceful	Schedule a meeting to discuss the strengths of team members and consider how we can modify roles and responsibilities around these. Determine how support staff can be better aligned around new priorities.
Perseverance	Schedule additional meetings to workshop the critical obstacles ahead. Include a shared lunch and informal catch up time. Ensure a united front of positivity and optimism, with concerns being discussed in private. Respond promptly to negativity from staff.

R@W Team Component	Action plan
Self-care	Recognise that we have a hard road ahead and will need to be more mindful of supporting each other. Ensure holidays are booked in advance. Minimise out-of-hours contact. Have walk and talk meetings. Provide healthy food at meetings. Share each other's stress management strategies and encourage use of these.
Capability	Map the new networks we require for success and allocate responsibility for developing these. Seek feedback from the Board on team capabilities and potential development needs given the changes in direction.
Connected	Link each team member with a leadership coach to support them during the restructure. Develop inter-team projects to minimise silos. Use the Employee Assistance Service as a preventative measure to debrief and keep well-being on track.
Alignment	Pause to regularly review progress and communicate this to staff. Develop a skills matrix, with staff, to encourage cross training and knowledge sharing.

Sample plan 2

This situation is an example of where a service team needs intensive attention to restore resilience.

R@W Team Component	Action plan
Robust	Develop a team charter and agree on how to operationalise it. Focus on one aspect a month and review it during monthly meetings. Address bad behaviour by Jack (manager role).
Resourceful	Address under-performance of Jenny (manager role). Revisit work priorities and accountabilities. Develop a shared spreadsheet to track team progress. Change the way in which meetings are conducted. Allocate time to joint problem solving around concerns using mapping tools and a rotating Chair.
Perseverance	Engage a facilitator to run a session on the impact of negativity on personal well-being and performance. Include how to respond to negativity. Decrease time spent complaining and talking about concerns. Change the language used to describe the team's problems. Organise some opportunities to lighten up and have fun.
Self-care	Agree on breaks and departure times. Link members not managing pressure into support via the Employee Assistance Service.

R@W Team Component	Action plan
Capability	Gain feedback from customers on team performance and develop a plan to action comments made.
Connected	Detail expectations in relation to support within the team. Determine the support needed for each team member and link accordingly (e.g. mentor, skill training, counselling). Develop shared projects with clear accountability.
Alignment	Arrange for mediation between Meryl and Martin (manager role). Coach each other to be more tolerant around differences.

Teams in trouble

If your team is experiencing major problems then you will need to invest heavily in restoring function before building resilience. This will need intensive input. Develop a multi-level plan and implement a number of actions simultaneously. A drip feed approach, trying one or two strategies at a time, is unlikely to have sufficient impact.

Consider getting independent expertise to assist you. A systemic approach is best which means having a plan for team members individually, the team overall and processes and structures that will support the behavioural shifts needed. This requires a sound diagnosis of the sources of dysfunction, rather than a focus on alleviating symptoms. This is why expert advice is recommended.

Reviewing your team plan

Throughout this book we have emphasised that resilience is not fixed. It is neither an attribute that we can claim nor a destination we have arrived at. Resilience is a dynamic state that constantly changes as the environment around us shifts and we need to re-orient our R@W toolkit accordingly.

This means that your team's plan will need regular review if you want to give yourselves the best chance of sustaining both your performance and health.

Your team's resilience will always be a work in progress.

 Top Tips

Build on what works well

Include maintenance of current team actions in your plan as sometimes you don't appreciate what you have until it's gone.

Tweak your plan regularly

Staying resilient involves deploying your toolkit differently as new challenges are faced. You may need to swap your spanner for a hammer, or use both when circumstances change.

Know when you are out of your depth

When you are immersed in the problem it can be harder to see solutions. Recognise when you need external help, and be willing to request it.

Chapter 13

Leading for resilience

When you are a leader, whether you like it or not, you have a significant influence on the work climate within your team. The power implicitly assigned to your management role provides the opportunity to shape others' behaviour, without even trying. It also helps define the unwritten rules around how the team operates – its culture.

If you want to promote resilience within the team(s) that you lead you need to think about how you:

- Overtly role model resilience
- Create space for discussion and planning around resilience
- Determine what you need to personally do, as the leader, to support the resilience of your team.

If you have worked through this book with your staff, you will have already identified ways to support them. This chapter provides the opportunity for additional personal reflection from a leadership perspective. Of course, any actions you decide to implement need to be consistent with the plan developed by your staff. Integrating strategies at the leader level as well as the individual and team level is integral to the systemic approach advocated in Chapter 2.

Role modelling resilience

Before you can make any requests of your team you need to get your own house in order. Start by working on your own resilience. Ideas on how to do this are contained in the book *Building Your Resilience: How to Thrive in a Challenging Job* (Appendix B).

Effective leaders do what they expect others to do. It's typically described in workplaces as 'leading by example'. As with parenting, it is what you do not what you say that matters.

If you encourage your staff to go home on time but consistently stay late yourself, the message is mixed. The unsaid communication is more likely to be that you need to routinely work after hours to get ahead.

If you are a team leader who readily offers support but does not seek it, or take it when offered, the unwritten message is that you cope on your own and so should they.

Creating resilience in the teams you lead

The model used to lead with resilience is the R@W Leader component of the R@W Toolkit (Appendix A). It outlines what you need to do as a manager to support the seven components needed for resilience within a team.

As outlined in Chapter 2, leaders can be resilient at the cost of those who report to them and leave a trail of fall-out in their wake. Here we promote a style of leadership that fosters team well-being, as well as performance. It is team rather than self-focused.

How to use this section

This section provides an opportunity for you to examine the extent to which you lead in a way that creates resilience within your team or teams.

The techniques are applicable to any level of leadership – whether you are the chairperson of a board, an executive, middle manager or front-line leader.

For each of the seven R@W Team components you are asked to consider the following activities:

1. Create the Vision

Develop a vision of what it would look like if your staff were investing in each component. You may choose to think about this, or relax, close your eyes and visualise it. You could try this exercise alone or with your team.

2. Reflect on your responses to key questions

A number of questions are posed on aspects of each component. Consider your answers to these before undertaking the next step.

3. Self-assess your current performance

Rate your leadership from 0-6 on the component, where a rating of 6 is performing at an exemplary level and 0 indicates that it rarely happens. Once you have completed the rating, summarise what you are doing that has led you to rate yourself in this way. This is an important part of the exercise as it prompts you to consider what you actually do, or don't do.

4. Determine the actions you want to take

For the final step, outline what you need to do to feel that you have moved up one rating. For example, if you assessed yourself at 3, what could you initiate to rate yourself at 4? Then, determine your commitment to taking action, the next step(s) you need to take and your approach to obstacles that you think may arise.

Committing to a number of small next steps on each component, as relevant to your situation, will make a large difference over time.

Note that it is not important to have actions for all of the areas, since not all of them will be of equal importance for your team. There may also be organisational constraints that make change difficult to implement in some areas. While you may not be able to address these constraints at the moment, being more mindful of them will allow you to notice opportunities that may arise as the team's circumstances change.

🔗 T1 Robust

Having shared purpose, goals and values and the skills needed to do the job.

Being proactive when issues arise for the team.

Visualising the robust team

Imagine, in your mind's eye, your team being aligned with purpose, values and goals as well as being quick to resolve obstacles that get in the way of this. Observe:

- The words they are using and the passion and energy they are showing when they talk about what is to be done and why
- The way in which they are interacting and the respect and trust they are demonstrating with each other
- How they work together to address issues promptly.

Picture this happening in everyday interactions - at meetings, in private conversations and in communication with customers.

What does this look, sound and feel like? What exists already, and what is missing in your team to achieve this vision?

Questions to ask yourself

Questions to reflect on:

- Does my team have a clear purpose and how well do I communicate this?
- How well do I link our goals and activities to the 'why'?
- What are the values that underlie the culture we want in our team and what am I doing to communicate these and help the team to live them?
- How well am I demonstrating the values I want from others?
- How proactive am I in addressing behaviours not aligned with what we expect?
- How well am I assisting my team in calling behaviours that are inconsistent with what we want?
- How do I support the team to address problems that arise?

Your self-assessment

My rating from 0-6 on this aspect is:.............

I have given myself this rating because:

Actions to take

What do I personally need to start to do, or change, to move up one rating?

Am I going to do this?

What could get in the way and how do I approach this?

What is the next step(s) I need to take?

⊕ T2 Resourceful

Harnessing team member strengths and resources and building a culture of continuous improvement.

Developing effective team processes that enable a clear focus on priorities.

Visualising the resourceful team

Imagine that a miracle has happened overnight and you arrive at work to see a fully resourceful team that is energised by change and fully using every resource they have available. Notice how they:

- Galvanise their personal strengths to full advantage
- Share everything available to them in order to meet their goals
- Are each accountable for their contribution
- Thrive on looking at ways to do things better.

Picture this happening in everyday interactions – when planning work, when budgets are cut and when change is needed.

What does this look, sound and feel like? What exists already, and what is missing in your team to achieve this vision?

Questions to ask yourself

Questions to reflect on:

- How well am I promoting the best use of the resources we have?
- Are my team members conversant with each other's strengths and are these being used to maximum advantage?
- Have I created processes that allow us to regroup and ensure we are focusing energy on the important areas?
- What am I doing to create an environment where we regularly explore how we can better perform our job?
- What am I doing to make change something we embrace?
- How well do I manage a lack of accountability by members?

Your self-assessment

My rating from 0-6 on this aspect is:............

I have given myself this rating because:

Actions to take

What do I personally need to start to do, or change, to move up one rating?

Am I going to do this?

What could get in the way and how do I approach this?

What is the next step(s) I need to take?

⚡ T3 Perseverance

Staying optimistic and having a solution, rather than a problem, focus.

Persisting in the face of obstacles.

Visualising a team with perseverance

Close your eyes and visualise your team optimistically persisting during a challenging time. Notice how they:

- Re-group and look for solutions together
- Maintain perspective, keep smiling and make time for fun and laughter
- Take turns in energising the team.

Picture this happening in everyday interactions – when setbacks occur, when persistence is needed and when negativity is the easiest option.

What does this look, sound and feel like? What exists already, and what is missing in your team to achieve this vision?

Questions to ask yourself

Questions to reflect on:

- To what extent do I demonstrate and create optimism and positive energy in my team?
- What could we savour more in our job?
- How do I engender a solution-focused approach to problems we are facing?
- What sort of language do I use in relation to problems?
- How well do I assist the team in dealing with negativity?
- Where does the energy come from in my team for persistence? How can I foster this?

Your self-assessment

My rating from 0-6 on this aspect is:............

I have given myself this rating because:

Actions to take

What do I personally need to start to do, or change, to move up one rating?

Am I going to do this?

What could get in the way and how do I approach this?

What is the next step(s) I need to take?

♥ T4 Self-care

Promoting and deploying good stress management routines and being alert to overload in members.

Supporting life-work balance.

Visualising a team with a culture of self-care

Picture your team working through a very busy period while still taking care of their well-being. Notice how they are:

- Checking in with each other to make sure they are okay
- Taking breaks, eating properly and ensuring there are opportunities to de-stress, share the load or debrief
- Being mindful of working hours and the impact on personal lives.

Picture this happening in everyday interactions – when deadlines are tight, the workload is high and home demands are competing.

What does caring for personal well-being look, sound and feel like? What exists already, and what is missing in your team to achieve this vision?

Questions to ask yourself

Questions to reflect on:

- How well do I look after my own well-being?
- Have I worked with my team on techniques to manage the stress we experience and boundaries we need to put in place for life-work balance?
- How alert am I to symptoms of overload in my staff and what do I do about it? What do I encourage others to do about it?

187

Your self-assessment

My rating from 0-6 on this aspect is:............

I have given myself this rating because:

Actions to take

What do I personally need to start to do, or change, to move up one rating?

Am I going to do this?

What could get in the way and how do I approach this?

What is the next step(s) I need to take?

✅ T5 Capability

Continually building capacity through accessing networks and supports. Seeking feedback and building on what works well.

Visualising capability

Visualise your team continually building its capability to meet shifting demands. Observe how people are:

- Responsive to the changing needs of stakeholders
- Building relationships with people outside of the team who can add value to the group's work.

Picture a team that is well connected, links well into other resources and continually builds its capacity to do its job. Observe who are they talking to, how this is initiated and when they do this.

What does it look, sound and feel like if your team is connected? What exists already, and what is missing in order to achieve this vision?

Questions to ask yourself

Questions to reflect on:

- How do I work with my team to identify the external relationships and supports we need?
- How well do I demonstrate the need to connect strategically with people outside of our team?
- What else can we do to make sure we get the feedback we need to make sure we stay on track and meet the needs of our stakeholders?

Your self-assessment

My rating from 0-6 on this aspect is:............

I have given myself this rating because:

Actions to take

What do I personally need to start to do, or change, to move up one rating?

Am I going to do this?

What could get in the way and how do I approach this?

What is the next step(s) I need to take?

👥 T6 Connected

Caring for colleagues as people and being co-operative and supportive with each other.

Visualising a connected team

Picture a team where members care for and support each other; where it's acceptable to be vulnerable and seek assistance; and where people feel that they belong and that they matter.

Observe how they:

- Help each other without needing to be asked
- Readily ask when they require assistance
- Encourage a feeling of belonging to the group
- Know and care about each other on a personal level.

Imagine someone joining the team. Notice what team members do and say to make this person feel welcome. How do they ensure they are supported and valued and how does this translate into how people typically interact?

What does a connected team look, sound and feel like? What exists already, and what is missing in your team to achieve this vision?

Questions to ask yourself

Questions to reflect on:

- What am I doing to encourage belonging within our team, and within the organisation as a whole?
- What do we do to get to know each other on a personal level? How well do I know my staff?
- How do I encourage mutual support within my team? What could I do, and what discussions could I facilitate? How do I support others and could I do this better?
- How do I instil an environment where it is okay, or even expected, to ask for help?

Your self-assessment

My rating from 0-6 on this aspect is:............

I have given myself this rating because:

Actions to take

What do I personally need to start to do, or change, to move up one rating?

Am I going to do this?

What could get in the way and how do I approach this?

What is the next step(s) I need to take?

👍 T7 Alignment

Aligning and developing the talents of team members to create the desired outcomes.

Sharing and celebrating success with each other.

Visualising an aligned team

Visualise your team being fully aligned in their effort, sharing their knowledge, acknowledging the contributions of each other and celebrating success. Picture team members that:

- Have a shared version of how they are adding value
- Recognise individual effort and celebrate success together
- Readily share what they know
- Promptly resolve conflict between them so that it doesn't get in the way of teamwork.

Picture this happening when there are few good news stories and when there is potential for competition and conflict.

What does an aligned team look, sound and feel like? What exists already, and what is missing in your team to achieve this vision?

Questions to ask yourself

Questions to reflect on:

- How well do we assess progress in our work and what do I do to communicate and highlight this?
- What does success look like for us and how do we build in celebrations of our achievements?
- How well is interpersonal conflict managed? How clear are the processes and my role in it?
- Are my staff sufficiently empowered or skilled in having difficult conversations?
- To what extent am I facilitating sharing of knowledge and skills?

Your self-assessment

My rating from 0-6 on this aspect is:............

I have given myself this rating because:

Actions to take

What do I personally need to start to do, or change, to move up one rating?

Am I going to do this?

What could get in the way and how do I approach this?

What is the next step(s) I need to take?

Comparing your views

Now that you have reflected on your leadership, rated yourself on each component and assessed what you may need to do, you may feel brave enough to seek feedback from one or two members of your team.

Would they rate you more favourably, less favourably or in the same way?

The easiest way to find out is to ask them to conduct the rating exercise you have just undertaken. Ask them to rate you on each element and outline what led them to rate you in that way.

While this section is focused on leadership of your team, it is likely that you a member of multiple teams, including with the person your report to.

How would you rate your manager and how can you influence him or her to act in a way to better build resilience within the leadership team you are part of?

⚙ Top Tips

Walk the talk

You cannot expect others to invest in their resilience unless you lead the way.

Create space for team planning and action

When there are plenty of tasks to do, it is unlikely that resilience will be given any attention unless you create the space and motivation to focus on it.

Contribute to all of the teams you belong to

You don't have to be the assigned leader to take the initiative. Influence all of the groups that you are part of. It will ultimately make your life easier.

A final thought

If you always do what you've always done,
you will always get what you've always got.

With the pace of change around you, what are
the consequences of doing nothing differently?

| Appendix A

Resilience at Work® Toolkit

The R@W Toolkit is a complementary suite of scales that recognises the interrelatedness of employee, leader and team resilience at work. The scales can be used independently or together, depending on your needs.

RESILIENCE AT WORK (R@W) TOOLKIT

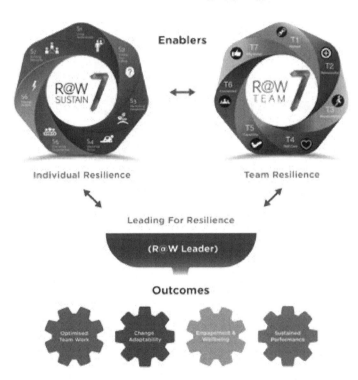

R@W® Scale (Individual) - A measure based on the Sustain 7 Model that assesses individual employee resilience. This comprises seven components as shown in Figure 6 on the next page.

Figure 6: Resilience at Work® Scale (Individual)

R@W® Team Scale. A measure that assesses group practices that promote resilience. This builds on the R@W Individual Scale and can be used when there is an opportunity to work with the whole team.

The R@W Team measures the seven components covered in this book.

R@W Leader® Scale. A measure that assesses the leader behaviours that support and foster resilience in employees and teams. This can be used as a stand-alone measure in coaching and leadership development, or together with the complete R@W Toolkit.

The R@W Leader measures the extent to which leaders support teams in the seven components of the R@W Team. It comprises self and team member ratings.

For more information see www.workingwithresilience.com.au

| Appendix B

Other Books by Kathryn McEwen

Building Your Resilience: How to Thrive in a Challenging Job

Published by Mindset Publications. South Australia 2016

This book will help you to formulate a plan to perform optimally at work while keeping your personal well-being intact. It is useful if you are:

- Regularly dealing with difficult tasks or demanding customers
- Working in constant change and uncertainty
- Part of a team with difficult group dynamics or limited effectiveness
- Time pressured or having to do more with less budget and less staff
- Finding it hard to have a life outside of work
- Dealing with a difficult boss, or
- Keeping your head above water yet looking for an extra boost to your resilience.

It is based on the R@W Sustain 7 model that comprises seven components critical for work resilience. The book contains lots of practical ideas and case studies and complements *Building Team Resilience* as it focuses on individuals, as opposed to the group overall.

Building Resilience at Work

Published by Australian Academic Press. Queensland 2011

This book takes a holistic approach through exploring how to develop personal resilience at work emotionally, mentally, physically and spiritually. It has a plethora of proven strategies for individuals and teams that are different, but complementary, to those covered in this book and *Building Your Resilience: How to Thrive in a Challenging Job*

Short Poppies Can Grow: Confidence at Work

Co-authored with psychologist Jacky Dakin

Published by Mindset Publications. South Australia 2009

A critical aspect of resilience is a good level of personal confidence and what psychologists label 'self-efficacy' – a belief that you are able to achieve the goals you set. This book is an excellent self-help guide to building confidence in the workplace. It provides a wealth of ideas and strategies to use across a variety of typical work scenarios. It can help you:

- Make an impact
- Speak out at meetings
- Deal with difficult colleagues
- Persist during tough times
- Take criticism on the chin
- Overcome nerves
- Sell your ideas and influence others
- Move out of your comfort zone or
- Get the job you want.

You can purchase these books on-line at
www.workingwithresilience.com.au

Made in the USA
San Bernardino, CA
26 February 2020